FOURTH GRADE

TIMBERDOODLE'S CURRICULUM HANDBOOK

2020–2021 NONRELIGIOUS EDITION

"ROBOT" COVER ART BY HOLLY, AGE 4
"FARM FRIENDS" COVER ART BY AUDREY, AGE 11
ALL THE GORGEOUS INTERIOR DOODLES PROVIDED BY OUR TALENTED CUSTOMERS

©2020 Timberdoodle Company, Second Edition
All rights reserved. Photocopying and digital reproduction permitted by and for use of the original purchasing family only.

Welcome to **Fourth Grade**

WE'RE SO GLAD YOU'RE HERE!

Congratulations on choosing to homeschool this year! Whether this is your first year as a teacher or your tenth, we're confident you'll find that there is very little that compares to watching your child's learning take off. In fact, teaching can be quite addictive, so be forewarned!

ON YOUR MARK, GET SET, GO!

Preparing for your first "school day" is very easy. Peruse this guide, look over the typical schedule, browse the introductions in your books, and you will be ready to go.

GET SUPPORT

Are you looking for a place to hang out online with like-minded homeschoolers? Do you wonder how someone else handled a particular science kit? Or do you wish you could encourage someone who is just getting started this year? Join one or more of our Facebook groups.

Timberdoodlers of all ages:
https://www.facebook.com/groups/Timberdoodle/

Timberdoodlers with 1st- to 4th-grade students:
www.facebook.com/groups/ElementaryTimberdoodle

Timberdoodlers using nonreligious kits:
https://www.facebook.com/groups/SecularTimberdoodle

SCHEDULE CUSTOMIZER

Your 2020-2021 Fourth-Grade Nonreligious Curriculum Kit includes access to our Schedule Customizer where you can not only adjust the school weeks but also tweak the checklist to include exactly what you want on your schedule. To get started, just click the link in your access email and visit the scheduling website!
www.TimberdoodleSchedules.com

If you ordered through a charter school or don't have that link for some other reason, just email schedules@Timberdoodle.com and we'll get that sorted out ASAP. (Including your order number will really speed that process up for you.)

WE WILL HELP

We would love to assist you if questions come up, so please don't hesitate to contact us with any questions, comments, or concerns. Whether you contact us by phone, email, or live online chat, you will get a real person who is eager to serve you and your family.

YOU WILL LOVE THIS!

This year, you and your student will learn more than you hoped while having a blast. Ready? Have an absolutely amazing year!

CONTENTS

INTRODUCTORY MATTERS

07	Meet Your Handbook
08	Tips & Tricks
12	Ask Your Fourth-Grader
14	Meet Your Online Scheduler
18	Annual Planner
19	What Is a Lesson?
22	Sample Weekly Checklists

THE READING CHALLENGE

24	Your Reading Challenge
28	Reading Challenge Charts
90	549 Book Suggestions
110	Book Awards & Party

YOUR KIT'S COMPONENTS

34	Language Arts
40	Mathematics
43	Thinking Skills
47	History & Social Studies
52	Science
56	STEM Learning
59	Art
65	Learning Tools

ARTICLES

69	From Our Family to Yours
70	What Makes Games a Priority?
72	Why Emphasize Independent Learning?

74	9 Reasons to Stop Schoolwork and Go Build Something!
76	What If This Is Too Hard?
78	9 Tips for Homeschooling Gifted Children
80	Convergent & Divergent Thinking
82	Help! My Book Says "Common Core"!

ITEM-BASED RESOURCES

84	Mosdos Ruby Weekly Assignments

WHEN YOU'RE DONE HERE

112	Your Top 4 FAQ About Next Year
114	Doodle Dollar Reward Points

MEET YOUR HANDBOOK

WELCOME TO YOUR TEACHING TOOLBOX!

Simple Is Better
We really believe that, so your guide is as simple as we could make it.

1. The Planning
First up are all the details on planning your year, including your annual planner and sample weekly checklists, the absolute backbones of Timberdoodle's curriculum kits. More on those in a moment.

2. Reading Challenge
Next up is the reading challenge, complete with book ideas to give you a head start.

3. Item-by-Item Details
We include short bios of each item in your kit, ideal for refreshing your memory on why each is included or to show off exactly what your fourth-grader will be covering this year. This is where we've tucked in our tips or tricks to make this year more awesome for all of you.

4. Teacher Resources
In this section, you'll find our favorite articles and tidbits amassed in our more-than-30 years of homeschool experience.

5. Items with Special Instructions and Book Suggestions
This is where you'll find your week-by-week schedule for Mosdos.

6. Book Suggestions
Finally, we'll conclude with specific book ideas for your reading challenge this year.

All the Details Included
This Timberdoodle curriculum kit is available in two different standard levels: Complete or Elite. This allows you to choose the assortment best suited to your child's interest level, your family's schedule, and your budget. In this guide, you'll find an overview and any tips for each of the items included in the Elite Curriculum Kit. If you purchased a Complete kit, or if you customized your kit, you chose not to receive every item, so you'll only need to familiarize yourself with the ones which were included in your kit.

Don't Panic, You Didn't Order Too Much Stuff!
We know you. OK, maybe not you personally, but we have yet to meet a homeschooler who doesn't have other irons in the fire. From homesteading or running a business to swimming lessons or doctor's appointments, your weeks are not dull. As you unpack your box you may be asking yourself how you'll ever fit it all in.

We'll go in-depth on schedules momentarily, but for now, know that most of the items in your kit feature short lessons, not all of them should be done every day, and your checklist is going to make this incredibly manageable. Really!

TIPS & TRICKS

YOUR FIRST WEEK, STATE LAWS, AND MORE

Week 1 Hints
As you get started this year, realize that you are just getting your sea legs. Expect your studies to take a little longer and be a little less smooth than they will be by the end of the year. As you get your feet under you, you will discover the rhythm that works best for you! If you don't know where to begin each day, why not try starting with something from the Thinking Skills category? It will get your child's brain in gear and set a great tone for the rest of the day.

Find Your Pace
We asked parents who used this kit how long their students spent on "school." Most said that they spent 3–5 hours per day, 4–5 days a week. That is not only a wide variation, but it also means some were outside that window. Make sure you allow yourself and your child some time to find your own rhythm!

Books First, or Not?
Some goal-oriented students might like to start each day with bookwork and end with fun, hands-on time. Others might prefer to intersperse the hands-on thinking games, STEM, and so forth between more intensive subjects to give their brains a clean slate.

A Little Every Day, or All at Once?
Depending on your preferences, your child's attention span, and what other time commitments you have (teaching other children, doctor appointments, working around a baby's nap), there are many different ways to schedule your week. Some families like to do a little portion from nearly all subjects every day, while others prefer to blast out an entire week's work within a subject in a single sitting. Throughout the year, you can tinker around with your daily scheduling and see what approach works best for your family.

Tips for Newbies
If you're new to homeschooling, it might be helpful for you to know that some subjects are typically taught and practiced several times a week for the best mastery. These would include basic math instruction, phonics, and spelling. However, more topical subjects such as geography, history, and science

are often taught all at once. Meanwhile, thinking skills, STEM, and art, plus hands-on learning and games, can be even more tailored to the preferences of the child or used for independent learning while you are busy.

What About the Courses Which You Don't Work on Every Week?

As you go over your checklist, you'll notice that some of your courses are "2–3 a month" or "as desired," and that may leave you confused on how to tackle them. Here are a few options: You could go ahead and do it every week, completing the course early. You could set aside the item for summer (see below). Or you could complete it as directed, of course!

The Summer Plan

If you're looking at all these tools and feeling a little overwhelmed, or if you just wish you had more structured activities for the summer, feel free to grab a handful of items from the kit and set them aside for summer. Then, set a reminder on your phone or calendar to remind you which ones they are and where you stashed them so you won't forget to use them!

Continued on the next page.

TIPS & TRICKS, CONT.

Meeting State Requirements
Check https://www.hslda.org/laws to see the most current information on your specific requirements. For many states, it is sufficient to simply hang on to your completed and dated weekly checklists along with a sampling of your child's best work this year. Some states ask you to add in a state-specific topic or two, such as Vermont history, or a generic course like P.E. or health. We have a summary on our blog comparing your kit to their requirements, but HSLDA is the gold standard for current legal information.

P.E.? Health?
We suggest thinking outside the box on this. Many of the science courses have a health component that meets the requirement. P.E. is a great way to fit your child's favorite activity into the school schedule. Ballet, soccer, horseback riding, swimming… there are so many fun ways to check off P.E. this year!

Put Your Child in Charge?
The weekly checklists are the framework of your week, designed for maximum flexibility. Just check off each item as you get it done for the week, and you'll be able to see at a glance that you still need to do _____ this week. (This is true of the daily checklists, as well–just on a shorter schedule.) Many students even prefer to get all their work done early in the week and enjoy all their leisure time at once!

10   www.timberdoodle.com • ©2020

Do Hard Things and Easy Ones

Our family provides foster care for kids who need a safe place for a while. This has exposed us to a whole new world of hard days and stressful weeks. If your child is struggling today, you are not failing if you take a step back and have him start with his most calming project. For our crew, often that would be art or the reading challenge. You even have a little slush room in most subjects, so don't hesitate to trim the lessons short on a busy or challenging week. You might even pause schoolwork today for a complete reset and tackle it fresh tomorrow.

At the same time, you are not doing your child any favors if you never teach him how to work through a challenge. After all, you have hard days as a parent and still get up, drink your coffee, and jump back in. Be aware of your own tendency to have your child either buckle down and push through or ease off completely, then work to provide a healthy balance for your child, particularly if he is in the process of healing.

Pro Tip

When you first get out a week's checklist, go ahead and check off all the things you don't need to do this week. For instance, if your child did a few extra pages of math last week or you are putting off all art kits until winter, check those off. Doesn't that feel better?

The Sample Schedules

We're including a sample annual planner on page 18, followed by sample weekly planners for each level of your kit, reflecting a typical 36-week school year. This lets you see at a glance how this might work for you, even before you get a moment to sit down at your computer and print your own custom-fitted schedule.

Ask Your Fourth-Grader!

A JUST-FOR-FUN BEGINNING OF THE YEAR INTERVIEW

Jot down your child's answers here to capture a fun timecapsule of his fourth-grade year.

1. What kind of thing would you want to invent if you were an inventor?

2. Where would you go if you could go anywhere you wanted in the world? Why?

3. What is something you look forward to doing when you grow up: drive a car, do a special sport...?

4. If you could lead an expedition, what kind of expedition would it be and where would it take you?

5. Have you ever looked through a telescope? If so, what kind of thing or place were you looking at?

6. Your ship is likely to sink at sea. What's in your emergency kit?

7. If you were going to design a toy or object to play with, what would it be?

8. What problem do you want to solve when you grow up?

A SELF-PORTRAIT (OR PHOTO) OF _____

MEET YOUR ONLINE SCHEDULER

GETTING THE MOST OUT OF YOUR PLANNERS

Use the Customizer
On the next pages, you'll find sample weekly checklists for the Complete and Elite kits. Before you photocopy 36 of them, though, take a moment to check out the custom online schedule builder that came free with your kit. You'll not only easily adjust the weeks, but you'll also tweak the checklist to include exactly what you want listed. Plus, you'll be able to print your weekly checklists directly from the schedule builder so you don't have to do that by photocopying! www.TimberdoodleSchedules.com

Activating Your Account
Before you can get started, you'll need your account activated for the online schedule builder. If you didn't get an activation email (perhaps you ordered through a charter school so we didn't have your email address), shoot us a quick email at schedules@Timberdoodle.com and we'll get that straightened out ASAP. Including your order number really speeds that process up, but our team is skilled at finding your activation info with whatever order data you have.

What's Your Dream Schedule?
Now that you're ready, you'll want to know two things:

1. How Many Weeks Do You Want to Do School?
A standard school year is 36 weeks + breaks. Some families prefer to expedite and complete the entire year in fewer weeks—a great option for those of you who'd like to get all this year's school done before baby arrives, for instance. Or perhaps your family, like ours, prefers to school year-round and keep that brain sharp.

2. What Breaks Do You Want?

Thanksgiving, Christmas, winter break, spring break... you could also add in weeks off that you're traveling, have guests, baby is coming, or...

Typically you'll be adding full-week breaks only, so unless you're traveling to Disneyland® for little Beulah's birthday, you don't need to add that to the calendar. For single-day breaks, you'll likely prefer to just shuffle the work to earlier/later in the same week and keep on task otherwise. If you're using a daily schedule (next page), though, you may find it worth your time to enter days off, as well.

Choosing Your Items

Now just pop that data into the online schedule and scroll down to see the items you might have in your kit. Unchecking the boxes for any items you don't have removes them from your list. You'll also see "Alternative Items" listed under each subject. This usually includes all of our most popular customizations for this grade so that you can simply check a box and switch the scheduler to an upper or lower level math, for instance.

Add Custom Courses

Your course list is limited only by your imagination. Perhaps your friend wrote you a custom curriculum you'd like to include, your family makes up a band and you'd like to have practice on this list, or you need to list ballet since that's P.E. this year. At the very bottom of the page you'll find a place to add in just as many courses as you'd like. Just walk through the prompts on-screen to get it all set up.

Tweak It to Perfection

Do you have everything set? On the next screen you'll have some fun options.

Continued on the next page.

MEET YOUR ONLINE SCHEDULER, CONT.

1. Large-Font Edition
Want a large-font option? Just check the box. If you don't like how it looks, you can always come back and uncheck it.

2. Show Dates
Check this box if it's helpful for you to see at a glance that week 17 is January 13–17, for instance. Some teachers find this incredibly helpful while others prefer to move breaks around on the fly, making the dates irrelevant.

3. Weekly or Daily?
We prefer a weekly schedule, for the simple reason that our weeks are rarely without some anomaly. Off to the dentist's Tuesday? You won't fall behind by taking a day off.

Or perhaps you have Friday Robotics Camp for a couple of weeks and need to get all the week's work done over four days instead of five. No problem! This approach also teaches time-management skills (see the article on Independent Learning at the back of this book).

However, we've heard from many of you that having a daily schedule, especially for the first month, is a real life saver. So we developed one, and if it helps you, fantastic! The daily scheduler is programmed to split up the work as evenly as possible over the week, with the beginning of the week having any extra pages or lessons. (We all know that end-of-the-week doldrums are a real thing!)

Moving Courses to Certain Days
If you're opting for the daily scheduler, you do have some helpful fine-tuning options. Just click "Edit" on the course in question and you'll have the option of selecting on which days of the week the course will appear. This lets you do things like schedule history only on Wednesday because that is co-op day. Or, you could schedule science only on Tuesday or Thursday and STEM on Friday or Monday so that science and STEM are never on the same day.

Pro Tip
You can also opt to exclude an item from certain weeks. This is useful if you already know that you want to save an art kit for May so that Grandma can do it with Beulah, or if you don't want to break out the graphic novel until after Christmas since you've set it aside as a gift.

4. Show Unit Range?
This feature sounds so very data-y and not super helpful, but we think you just might love it. Instead of saying that you need to do seven pages of math this week, check this box to have it remind you that you're on worksheets 50–56 this week, for example. If you prefer extreme flexibility, leave this box unchecked. But if you're afraid of falling behind without knowing it, this box will be your hero.

Make More Lists
If you have one student and one teacher, you may feel free to buzz past this idea. But if you have an extra teacher–perhaps your spouse, a grandparent, or even an older sibling who wants the bonding time, then this may simplify your life! Instead of putting all of your child's work on a single list, you could put all the subjects you will teach on your list and all of the remaining subjects on "Grandma's list" for her ease.

If you have twins or multiple students at the same grade level, you can also make multiple lists to best meet each student's needs.

That's It!
Click Generate Schedule, then View Generated Schedule, and you're ready to print it and get started!

FYI, our scheduler is constantly being improved, so for the most current instructions, please refer to the blog link in your activation email.

Ideas Our Team Is Working On
At the time of this printing, our team is working to add a time log to these lists for those of you whose states require it. We're also adding a way to easily email the schedule to yourself for your record, adding a progress report, and fine-tuning how you add time off to your schedule. These are all features that you may expect to see more about on the afore mentioned blog. Also, please let us know if you think of more features that our team should consider!

Your Annual Planner

	CURRICULUM	LESSONS OR PAGES	= PER WEEK
Language Arts	Daily 6-Trait Writing	25 weeks	1 week's work
	Mosdos Literature Ruby	37 sub-sections	1 sub-section
	Spelling You See E	36 weeks	1 week's work
	First Language Lessons	85 lessons	2–3 lessons
Math	Math-U-See	30 lessons	a 7-worksheet lesson
	Extreme Dot-to-Dot: Farm Life	32 puzzles	1 puzzle
Thinking Skills	Building Thinking Skills 2	367 pages	10 pages
	ColorKu	100+ challenges	3 challenges
	Ultimo	unlimited	once a week
History & Social Studies	The Story of the World 4	42 chapters	1–2 chapters
	Skill Sharpeners Geography	132 pages	4 pages
	True Stories of War	3 books	unlimited
	24-Hour History	5 books	unlimited
Science	Building Blocks of Science	22 lessons	1 lesson
	Dr. Bonyfide 2	112 pages	3+ pages
STEM	Robotis Dream 2.0 Level 1 or Levels 1+2	12–24 lessons	1/2 or 1 lesson
	My Crazy Inventions Sketchbook	50 activities	1–2 activities
Art	Hey Clay Animals	6 animals	1 a month
	Djeco At Night	4 artboards	as desired
	Khan Mosaics	2 mosaics	as desired
	Pixel Mosaics	unlimited	20 minutes
	Write and Draw Your Own Comics	95 pages	3 pages
Etc.	Test Prep	128 pages	end of school year

www.timberdoodle.com • ©2020

WHAT IS A LESSON?

ITEM-BY-ITEM SPECS

On pages 34–68 you'll find an overview of each item, including information about how we split up the work and why, but if you're looking for a quick reference guide to refresh your mind on what exactly "one lesson" means for any of your materials, here you go!

Daily 6-Trait Writing
The course is split into 25 weeks of work. We suggest starting the one week's work per week pace after 11 weeks of school to allow you to ease into the year.

Mosdos Literature
The easiest way to use this course is to simply follow our suggested 36-week schedule starting on page 84 in this handbook.

It's probably worth noting here that we do suggest skipping the writing, though, since you'll be covering that with Daily 6-Trait. One thing to note: The unit on poetry has an extra lesson included.

Spelling You See
There are 36 lessons, each of which includes five days of work. Two tips: Your day's lesson is complete after 10 minutes of work—your child does not need to finish the whole chunk. Also, if you're using a four-day week or otherwise don't get to all five days of work in a week, it is expected that you will still count that lesson as complete at the end of the week and move to the next one.

First Language Lessons
In this book, the lessons are very clearly marked. Do two to three lessons per week (three for sure if you're planning to do the optional end lessons about writing letters, oral lessons, and dictionary skills).

Math-U-See
You'll find 30 lessons here, each with seven worksheets. Since you'll only be completing as many of the worksheets as your child needs per lesson, and since completing one whole lesson a week keeps the instructional portions predictable, we suggest doing one lesson a week instead of a certain number of worksheets. If you use that method, know that you can spread a tricky lesson over two weeks up to six times this year without messing up your schedule.

Extreme Dot-to-Dot
You'll want to do about one puzzle a week.

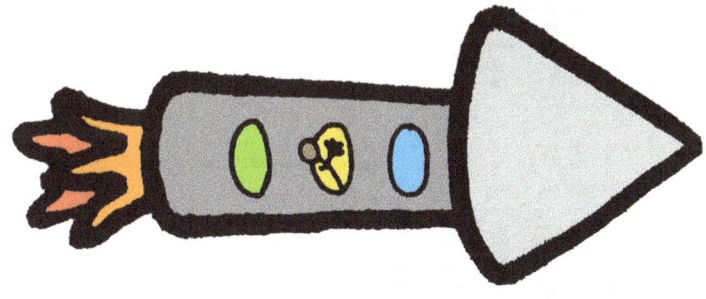

WHAT IS A LESSON? CONT.

Building Thinking Skills 2
You'll be working through this book at about 10 pages a week. Do keep in mind that this is used well as a one-or two-year course, so if this pace is overwhelming for your student, don't hesitate to drop back to five pages a week and use it for two years.

ColorKu
Just do three new challenges a week.

Ultimo
We suggest playing as many games as you'd like at least once a week.

The Story of the World 4
With 42 chapters, you're going to want to do 3 chapters every two weeks. Or, if it's easier, just do 2 chapters one week and 1 chapter the following week. Add in as many activities as you have the time/interest for.

Skill Sharpeners Geography
Simply doing four pages a week will get you through this year. Keep in mind that you're free to skip the writing assignments and elaborate activities if needed, but if your student has the time and energy, these will really serve to reinforce what he's learning.

True Stories of War
Time these either to be used with chapters 5, 20–21, and 28–29 of Story of the World, or release them to your child at any point for free reading. These books are captivating!

24-Hour History
These books cover the events addressed in Story of the World chapters 28, 29, 35, and 36 (two books for 36). You may either hang onto them until you reach those chapters or distribute them early like True Stories of War.

GeoCards
Unlimited. We suggest playing a game or two a week.

Building Blocks of Science
There are only 22 lessons in this text. We suggest completing one a week and finishing early or taking weeks off as desired. If you'd like a more precise number, doing two lessons every three weeks is a great pace. If you purchased the Elite kit, make sure you use your lab set for the easiest experiments ever!

Dr. Bonyfide
Just over three pages a week will take you through this year.

Robotis Dream 2.0 Levels 1 and 2
Each set has been designed as a 12-week course. If you got just Level 1, you could opt to complete 1/3 of a "week's work" every week to stretch the program out.

Or, if you received Levels 1 and 2, you are set up for 24 weeks of robotics. As with all of your work this year, feel free to blaze ahead if your student is ready for more!

My Crazy Inventions Sketchbook
There are 50 activities in this book, plus pages of brilliant or head-scratching inventions as inspiration. You'll want your child to read any informational pages he encounters and complete one or two activity pages each week, working straight through the book.

Hey Clay Animals
There are 6 happy and charming animals to build so we suggest completing roughly one a month. It will be best to build the entire animal at one time so that the clay adheres to itself, so try to pick a day where your child has a good chunk of time to work on it.

Djeco At Night
This set includes 4 artboards and scratch-art engraving instructions. Your student could work on them a little each week, or save them to complete on weeks he needs an indoor project.

Khan Mosaics
There are just two mosaics, yet each will take a fair bit of time to finish. Whittle away at it every week until completion, or save this kit for a long plane trip, a family gathering where the adults need quiet, or the 2021 Snowmageddon!

Pixel Mosaics
This set is unlimited. We suggest allotting at least 20 minutes a week.

Write and Draw Your Own Comics
With 95 pages in all, including the introductory matter, we suggest your child completes about 3 pages a week. Or have him complete 1 of the 24 chapters a week and anticipate finishing early. You could ask your child to use the remaining 12 weeks to turn in a weekly comic strip/story of his choosing.

Thinking Putty
Unlimited. We suggest making up at least one tin in the first week of school so that your child has a fidget handy.

Test Prep
We usually save this for the end of the year to refresh the student on all the skills he'll need for annual testing. You won't find this on your schedule unless you add it.

Weekly Checklist (Complete)

Subject	Resource	Weekly Goal
Language Arts	Daily 6-Trait Writing	1 week's work
Language Arts	Mosdos Literature Ruby	1 sub-section
Language Arts	Spelling You See	1 week's work
Language Arts	First Language Lessons	2–3 lessons
Math	Math-U-See	a 7-worksheet lesson
Thinking Skills	Building Thinking Skills 2	10 pages
Thinking Skills	ColorKu	3 challenges
History & Social Studies	The Story of the World 4	1–2 chapters
History & Social Studies	Skill Sharpeners Geography	4 pages
History & Social Studies	True Stories of War	unlimited
Science	Building Blocks of Science	1 lesson
Science	Dr. Bonyfide 2	3+ pages
STEM	Robotis Dream 2.0 Level 1	1/3 lesson
STEM	My Crazy Inventions Sketchbook	1–2 activities
Art	Hey Clay Animals	1 a month
Art	Djeco At Night	as desired

WEEKLY CHECKLIST (ELITE)

Language Arts	Daily 6-Trait Writing	1 week's work	☐	☐	☐	☐			
	Mosdos Literature Ruby	1 sub-section	☐						
	Spelling You See	1 week's work	☐	☐	☐	☐			
	First Language Lessons	2–3 lessons	☐	☐	☐				
Math	Math-U-See	a 7-worksheet lesson	☐	☐	☐	☐	☐		
	Extreme Dot-to-Dot: Farm Life	1 puzzle	☐						
Thinking Skills	Building Thinking Skills 2	10 pages	☐	☐	☐	☐	☐	☐	☐
	ColorKu	3 challenges	☐						
	Ultimo	once a week	☐						
History & Social Studies	The Story of the World 4	1–2 chapters	☐	☐					
	Skill Sharpeners Geography	4 pages	☐	☐					
	True Stories of War	unlimited	☐						
	24-Hour History	unlimited	☐						
Science	Building Blocks of Science	1 lesson	☐						
	Dr. Bonyfide 2	3+ pages	☐	☐	☐				
STEM	Robotis Dream 2.0 Levels 1 + 2	1 lesson	☐						
	My Crazy Inventions Sketchbook	1–2 activities	☐	☐					
Art	Hey Clay Animals	1 a month	☐						
	Djeco At Night	as desired	☐						
	Khan Mosaics	as desired	☐						
	Write and Draw Your Own Comics	3 pages	☐						

2020-2021 4th-Grade Nonreligious Curriculum Handbook • 800.478.0672

THE READING CHALLENGE

BASED ON THE READING CHALLENGE FOR KIDS FROM REDEEMEDREADER.COM

The Reading Challenge for Kids will get you and your child reading a broader variety of books this year and perhaps discovering new favorites. This reading challenge is heavily adapted by us and used with permission from the fine folks at RedeemedReader.com. Check out their website for more information about this reading challenge and for great book reviews and book suggestions for your kids.

Reading Solo and Together
At this grade level, it is likely that most of these books are titles he will read independently. However, we highly recommend keeping a read-aloud time, too, as long as it's possible. Many sources recommend that parents continue reading to their children well past the time their children become accomplished readers, and we agree!

How It Works

On the following pages, you'll find four lists of books which you are meant to read one after another this year. Not all families will make it through all the lists, so you will need to choose a reading goal early in the year and set your pace accordingly.

The Light Reader plan has 13 books, which sets a pace of 1 book every four weeks. The majority of families can and should do at least this much.

The Avid Reader plan adds another 13 books, which increases the pace to 1 book every two weeks. This is doable for most families.

The Committed Reader plan adds a further 26 books, bringing the total to 52, or 1 book every week. By including picture books, we think that even this faster pace is not too rigorous and is suitable for enthusiastic readers with time in their schedules.

The Obsessed Reader plan doubles the total yet again, bringing it to 104 books, which sets a pace of 2 books every week. We highly recommend this challenge, but it may be too intense for families with already-packed schedules!

Getting Started

Begin with the Light plan, which includes suggestions for 13 books. Choose those books and read them in any order, checking them off as you complete them.

Next, advance to the Avid plan, using the criteria there to choose another 13 books and read them in any order.

Then it's time to move to the Committed plan with a further 26 books, again reading them in any order.

If you have completed the Committed plan (that's 52 books so far!), you are ready to brave the Obsessed plan.

If you want to finish your books in a school year rather than in an entire calendar year, the timeline shifts a bit, so be sure to set your goal at the beginning of the year and pace yourself accordingly.

Here's the pace for a 36-week schedule:

Light Reader: One book every two to three weeks.
Avid Reader: One book every week or two.
Committed Reader: One and a half books every week.
Obsessed Reader: Almost three books every week.

How Long Do We Count Picture Books?

I recently heard this beautiful quote from Sarah Mackenzie at the Read-Aloud Revival:

"Another thing I want to point out is picture books. As your child grows older, do not stop reading picture books. Picture books are written, often times, with more eloquent, beautiful language than chapter books or middle-grade novels so the reading level in the picture book is actually higher than it is in the novel. A beautifully written picture book is like poetry and an art gallery combined into one. So they are not less than, or they're not inferior to longer novels. The beautiful thing about picture books is because they're short, you can experience more stories this way. So if you prioritize picture books over novels when it comes to reading aloud, you will actually fill your child's memories and childhood with more stories..." (Hear the whole conversation on the Read-Aloud Revival podcast, at the beginning of episode 121.)

THE READING CHALLENGE, CONT.

But I Don't Have Any Idea Which Books to Choose!
We have your back! Beginning on page 90 you'll find hundreds of book ideas you'll love this year.

If you want more ideas, we highly recommend your local librarian, the Read-Aloud Revival podcast, and the Timberdoodle Facebook groups as excellent starting points. It's also a wonderful idea to peek at the additional reading ideas in your history or science textbooks (particularly if your child was fascinated by something his courses recently touched on).

Will This Be Expensive?
It doesn't need to be. You can read library books, buy used, borrow from friends, and scour your family bookshelves. Don't forget that many libraries have free e-versions, as well.

It doesn't get much more convenient than that!

But How Do I Fit This Much Reading Into My Day?
Here are nine ideas to incorporate more reading into your family's busy schedule and unique schooling style:

1. Use Books of Various Lengths
A longer book than you'd usually pick may be perfect as an audio book. On the flip side, if your child will be be reading to a younger sibling or you are picking a new readaloud for the whole gang, feel free to gear the book towards the younger participants, particularly if you're short on time. Picture books allow for more stories in less time, but they don't lack at all for impact.

2. Assign Independent Reading
This can be done in conjunction with quiet time or simply throughout the day. Our household often uses it as a strategy to calm the hyper and soothe the sad—"I need you to go read one book (or one chapter) and then come back and we'll try again."

3. Quiet Time!
Does your family implement a quiet time already? Reading is a natural perk for that time. Quiet time can be as simple as setting a timer for 30 minutes (or more) and having your child relax with his favorite blanket or weighted lap pad and, of course, his book. If it's possible for you to grab a book that you've been wanting to read and embrace the same plan, you'll be modeling what an ageless wonder reading can be. Of course, if your household is filled with little ones, it may be more practical for you to use this time for feeding babies or fixing dinner and there's no shame in that, but consider

your options as you plan your year.

4. Sneak Reading Into Your Existing Routines
What routines are already going well for you? Could you incorporate a reading time right into your existing bedtime routine, car time, snack time, or other routine?

5. Audiobooks
Incorporate audiobooks and save the designated reader some time and energy. This is a particularly spectacular move for car time, art time, puzzle time, or even to smooth over particularly grumpy mealtimes.

6. Put the Busy Ones to Work
Encourage quiet activities such as puzzles, this year's STEM kit, or coloring while you read aloud or play the audiobook. It can be legitimately impossible for your kinesthetic learner to sit perfectly still and listen angelically, but break out the "listening time only" tools and suddenly everyone looks forward to reading!

7. Brothers and Sisters
You don't have to be the only one reading to your child. Have your "big kid" read to a younger sibling as part of their school lessons. The older sibling will gain fluency as your younger one soaks up the one-on-one time. (No younger ones in your home? How about cousins, playmates, grandparents, or even the family pet?)

8. Grandpa, Grandma, Aunties, Oh My!
Perhaps an auntie would welcome the opportunity to have Friday evenings be read-aloud time, complete with hot cocoa and scones. Or Grandma might love the idea of hosting all of her grandchildren once a month for a giant book party—each child could bring his favorite book to share. Too far away? Grandpa could record his favorite book (any audio-recording app should work), then send the book to your child so that he can read along with Grandpa.

9. Get a Library Routine Going
Our family has loved reading since our toddler days, but we didn't use the library well until we settled into a simple routine. For us that involves a central location for all library books and having a designated person willing to return current books and pick up the holds each week. Those simple steps have quickly borne fruit with many more hours spent reading "new" books!

Let's Read!
Pick your plan, choose some books with your child, and get started!

THE LIGHT READER

The Challenge	The Book You Chose	Date Completed
1. An inspirational book		
2. A book about the world		
3. A biography		
4. A classic novel/story		
5. A book your grandparent (or other relative) says was his/her favorite at your age		
6. A book about ancient history		
7. A book about something that makes you happy		
8. A book based on a true story		
9. A book that someone at least twice your age recommends		
10. A book more than 100 years old		
11. A book about families		
12. A book about relationships or friendship		
13. A book featuring someone of a different ethnicity than you		

THE AVID READER

The Challenge	The Book You Chose	Date Completed
14. A book about someone who came from another country		
15. A book of fairy tales or folk tales (or an extended retelling of one)		
16. A book recommended by a parent or sibling		
17. A book about the ocean		
18. A Caldecott, Newbery, or Geisel Award winner		
19. A book about a holiday		
20. A book about grandparents or senior citizens		
21. A book of puzzles		
22. A book that has a fruit in its title		
23. A book about a farm		
24. A book about illness or medicine		
25. A book about school, learning, or a teacher		
26. A graphic novel		

THE COMMITTED READER

The Challenge	The Book You Chose	Date Completed
27. A book of poetry		
28. A book with a great cover		
29. A book about food		
30. A book about weather		
31. A book about an adventure		
32. A book by or about William Shakespeare (or a retelling of one of his plays)		
33. A funny book		
34. A mystery or detective story		
35. A picture book		
36. A book by or about a famous American		
37. A book about Westward Expansion		
38. A book about the 20th-Century		
39. A book about money		

THE COMMITTED READER, CONT.

The Challenge	The Book You Chose	Date Completed
40. A book about art or artists		
41. A book about music or a musician		
42. A book about an invention or inventor		
43. A book of crafts or games		
44. A book about a boy		
45. A book about a girl		
46. A book about books or a library		
47. A book about adoption		
48. A book about someone who is differently abled (blind, deaf, mentally handicapped, etc.)		
49. A book you or your family owns but you've never read		
50. A book about babies		
51. A book about writing		
52. A book made into a movie (but read the book first!)		

THE OBSESSED READER

The Challenge	The Book You Chose	Date Completed
53. A book about your state or region		
54. A book recommended by a librarian or teacher		
55. An encyclopedia, dictionary, or almanac		
56. A book about building or architecture		
57. A biography of a world leader		
58. A book published the same year you (the student) were born		
59. A book with a one-word title		
60. A book or magazine about a career you're interested in		
61. A book about siblings		
62. A book about animals		
63. A book featuring a dog		
64. A book featuring a horse		
65. A book you have started but never finished		
66. A book about plants or gardening		
67. A book about a hobby or a skill you want to learn		
68. A book of comics		
69. A book about a famous war		
70. A book about sports		
71. A book about math (numbers, mathematicians, patterns…)		
72. A book about suffering or poverty		
73. A book by your favorite author		
74. A book you've read before		
75. A book with an ugly cover		
76. A book about someone's favorite subject		
77. A book about travel or transportation		
78. A book about the natural world		
79. A biography of an author		
80. A book published in 2020–2021		
81. A historical fiction book		

www.timberdoodle.com • ©2020

THE OBSESSED READER, CONT.

The Challenge	The Book You Chose	Date Completed
82. A book about science or a scientist		
83. A book about safety or survival		
84. A book about space or an astronaut		
85. A book set in Central or South America		
86. A book set in Africa		
87. A book set in Asia		
88. A book set in Europe		
89. A book with a color in its title		
90. A book about manners		
91. A book about spring		
92. A book about summer		
93. A book about autumn		
94. A book about winter		
95. A book from the 0–99 Dewey Decimal section of your library		
96. A book from the 100–199 Dewey Decimal section of your library		
97. A book from the 200–299 Dewey Decimal section of your library		
98. A book from the 300–399 Dewey Decimal section of your library		
99. A book from the 400–499 Dewey Decimal section of your library		
100. A book from the 500–599 Dewey Decimal section of your library		
101. A book from the 600–699 Dewey Decimal section of your library		
102. A book from the 700–799 Dewey Decimal section of your library		
103. A book from the 800–899 Dewey Decimal section of your library		
104. A book from the 900–999 Dewey Decimal section of your library		

LANGUAGE ARTS

PRACTICE MAKES PERFECT

Reading is probably the most important skill your child will practice this year. Whether he is a natural reader or one who doesn't truly enjoy reading, it is critical to make reading as fun and rewarding as possible now.

Our experience is that the best way to cultivate an eager reader is to constantly supply him with reading materials that interest him. Future doctors may want to read up on anatomy, young explorers are drawn to the escapades of adventurers young and old, and the child fascinated by babies will be captivated by adoption stories.

Knowing how hard it can be to load the whole family up and get to the library, we're also including a brilliant anthology of reading material in your Mosdos book this year. With so many excellent selections, every student is sure to find some that resonate deeply with him and others that he would never have chosen for himself but that he finds surprisingly interesting. Assign reading as needed, but encourage it at all costs; a child who enjoys reading will find it easier to excel in every area.

6-TRAIT WRITING
COMPLETE ~ ELITE

Are you familiar with trait writing? Trait-based writing is an impressive method educators have developed to determine whether a child's writing is skilled or not.

The six traits or characteristics that shape quality writing are content; organization; word choice; sentence fluency; voice; and conventions, which include grammar, spelling, and mechanics. It may sound ominous, but Daily 6-Trait Writing has made it effortless.

These short daily assignments are designed to build skills without being overwhelming. We love them for their brevity, but also because they are so thorough!

Scheduling
This is designed for one short lesson a day, ending after 25 weeks of school. If you prefer, you could opt to do only three to four days' work each week so that you don't finish too early. Most will likely wish to begin this on the 12th week of school and finish it with the rest of the materials, which will let you ease into the year.

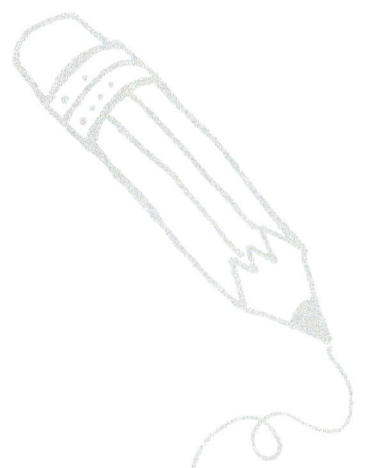

Mosdos Literature
COMPLETE ~ ELITE

Mosdos Literature is a complete literature program that cheerily reinforces the universal ideals of courage, honesty, loyalty, and compassion. We found this such a breath of fresh air in comparison to more "sensational" readers that glamorize evil or present subject matter that is not age-appropriate.

Mosdos Literature begins with the student reader which is beautifully illustrated using a generous amount of full-color photographs, color drawings, and black-and-white pictures.

Before each story in the student reader there is an introduction to the story and an explanation of some facet of literature. That literary focus can include character, theme, internal and external conflicts, setting, climax, foreshadowing, and more. This literary component is developed and illuminated through the stories. Vocabulary words that might be unfamiliar are presented in boxes on the pages where the words first appear in the account.

The stories are followed not just by the classic review questions designed to assess reading comprehension, but also by more complex questions that require thoughtful analysis. Every unit concludes with activities such as writing a short skit, doing a craft, or memorizing a poem. Pick the ones that best suit your child; there are far too many to do them all. Unless your child is a budding author, you can minimize the writing activities. Your child is already doing a lot of writing this year in Daily 6-Trait Writing and First Language Lessons.

Next is the consumable, colorful, and engaging Student Activity Workbook. For nearly every story in the student reader, the workbook contains corresponding vocabulary, creative writing, or comprehension questions, while also providing extended reinforcement of the literary elements being taught. These assignments help you to evaluate areas of progress or concepts that might require additional work.

The advantage of Mosdos Press is that the literature, vocabulary, and writing components all tie together, giving your child a chance to truly understand what was taught by approaching it in a variety of ways. (Again, you can totally skip the writing portions if your child isn't grooving on them this year. There is still so much to gain from the workbook and questions.)

Through great commentary plus questions and answers, the Teacher's Edition will make lively discussions with your child possible. Each page of the student reader is duplicated at a smaller size in the Teacher's Edition, yet it is still abundantly easy to read. Information is arranged in the ample margins around these replicated pages, discussing the literary components found in each story with clear, concise explanations. Of course, the Teacher's Guide also includes the answers for the Student Activity Workbook.

Scheduling

Complete one sub-section a week. Some may find it easiest to consider that a week's work will begin with the Lesson in Literature and include reading until you reach the next Lesson in Literature (unless it's a Lesson Wrap-up week).

A sample 36–week schedule is included on pages 84–89 for your convenience.

Complete the corresponding workbook pages, but do feel free to skip the creative writing assignments if that best serves your student.

Our family would have chosen to answer the Studying the Selection questions in the readers orally, and if time allowed, select one Focus or Creating and Writing activity to complete for further study. Other families may choose to complete every exercise included.

There are no workbook pages for the poetry unit, so in place of those, students may prioritize writing assignments from the Think About It section.

Busy families may choose to skip the Unit Wrap-ups, while others who enjoy the hands-on activities can complete them as desired.

SPELLING YOU SEE

COMPLETE ~ ELITE

This multisensory spelling program will help your child become a confident, successful speller, naturally and at his own speed. Because Spelling You See encourages visual memory rather than rote memory, there are no weekly spelling lists or tests and very little instructor preparation. Each daily lesson in Spelling You See: American Spirit uses real words presented in context within nonfiction stories about American history and culture.

Spelling You See: American Spirit is colorful, short, to the point, and fun!

Scheduling

The 36 weeks of work, with five daily activities each week, are already planned out for you. Just open and go!

ONE NOTE:

Ideally you will not complete more than one short spelling lesson every day for best retention. If your student is at all intimidated by the lesson length, keep in mind that there is enough work in each lesson to teach a speedy writer, but a more methodical writer could be overwhelmed trying to complete it all. Consider starting a timer for 10 to 15 minutes when you begin the day's work and stop where you are when it rings. The next day, just move on to the new lesson.

Also, if you do a four-day week, you only do the first four days' work and skip the fifth. It seems unusual to all of us who feel one must finish every page, but this course is designed to be most effective when used that way.

First Language Lessons
COMPLETE ~ ELITE

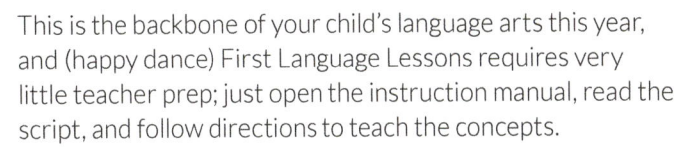

This is the backbone of your child's language arts this year, and (happy dance) First Language Lessons requires very little teacher prep; just open the instruction manual, read the script, and follow directions to teach the concepts.

The student workbook has appealing fonts and plenty of white space, so the individual pages are less intimidating for children. Do not be alarmed by the size of these books!

Each lesson is designed to take 30 minutes or less. In fact, the author suggests that if your student's lesson time exceeds 30 minutes, stop for the day, then continue with the remainder of the lesson the following day. Also, if a student is struggling to understand or if he doesn't write easily, he may do some of the written exercises orally instead.

By the time you've finished the course, you will have covered a full range of grammar topics, including parts of speech, punctuation, sentence diagrams, and skills in beginning writing and storytelling.

First Language Lessons' spiral learning method ensures mastery for every child, which is important for these foundational years of language study.

Does that seem like a lot for fourth grade? The premise of First Language Lessons is that students are almost always ready for more, if we will just take the time to teach them.

Scheduling

Do two to three lessons per week. If you choose to do the optional end lessons about contractions, writing letters, and dictionary skills, then plan on doing three lessons every week.

MATHEMATICS

MATH-U-SEE

Basic math is a critical skill for your child to master, whether he grows up to be a carpenter, doctor, accountant, or farmer. But all too often, math programs rely on memorization instead of comprehension, leaving the student at a disadvantage.

That's not going to happen to your child! The real-world math problems posed in Math-U-See (combined with the hands-on manipulatives) create an unbeatable math program.

With simple, uncluttered pages, Math-U-See is mastery-oriented, clear, to the point, and effective. In Math-U-See, new ideas are introduced step by step in a logical order, while concepts that have been mastered are reviewed periodically.

Math-U-See's teacher guide and supplemental DVD will teach more than just how to solve a math problem. They will also show why the problem is solved in this manner and when to apply the concept. On the DVDs, each lesson is demonstrated with kind-hearted enthusiasm. DVDs can be played on a DVD player or computer; however, Windows 10 users will need to download a separate video player.

MATH-U-SEE
COMPLETE ~ ELITE

While Math-U-See still requires a fair amount of parental involvement, by this grade your child will be able to work more independently. The instruction manual can be read by your child and, of course, he will want to watch the DVD presentation before beginning each lesson. The instruction manuals also include complete answers with step-by-step solutions for all the exercises and tests, and there is extra instruction for the enrichment problems.

Math-U-See is laid out with step-by-step procedures for introducing, practicing, mastering, and reviewing concepts. How do you know when your child has "mastered" a math concept? Not just when he gets the answers right, but when he can teach the concept back, especially if he is able to do so with a word problem. Math-U-See will show you how.

You will want to decide as you start the year whether your student will be completing the optional "Application and Enrichment" section of each lesson—sometimes considered the honors portion. If these challenges overwhelm your student, you should skip them or offer generous assistance. Otherwise, embrace them for the opportunity to help him learn more skills and train his brain to think logically.

It's worth mentioning that there are other reasons your child may not need to complete every one of these pages. At the risk of oversimplifying, the practice worksheets (A, B, C) are to be used with the manipulatives until your child reaches an "aha!" moment and grasps the lesson. He may then move to the review pages (D, E, F) and should at least complete worksheet D in its entirety. If he's breezing through the pages, you have several great options. One would be to have him complete every other problem, or he could skip E or F or both. (You do want to be sure he's not rusty on any of those problems before skipping, though—many students will do best completing all or most of the D, E and F worksheets.) Worksheet G is the application/enrichment/extra-credit page. It's okay to skip but valuable to complete.

Scheduling

You have 30 lessons to complete, so we suggest planning on 1 lesson a week, including the DVD as well as the textbook/workbook portions and any relevant tests. However, as Mr. Demme points out, some lessons will take you longer than others to achieve mastery. If you find yourself "stuck" on a lesson, feel free to allow it to take you an extra week. Just don't do that more than six times this year!

EXTREME DOT-TO-DOT
~~COMPLETE~~ ELITE

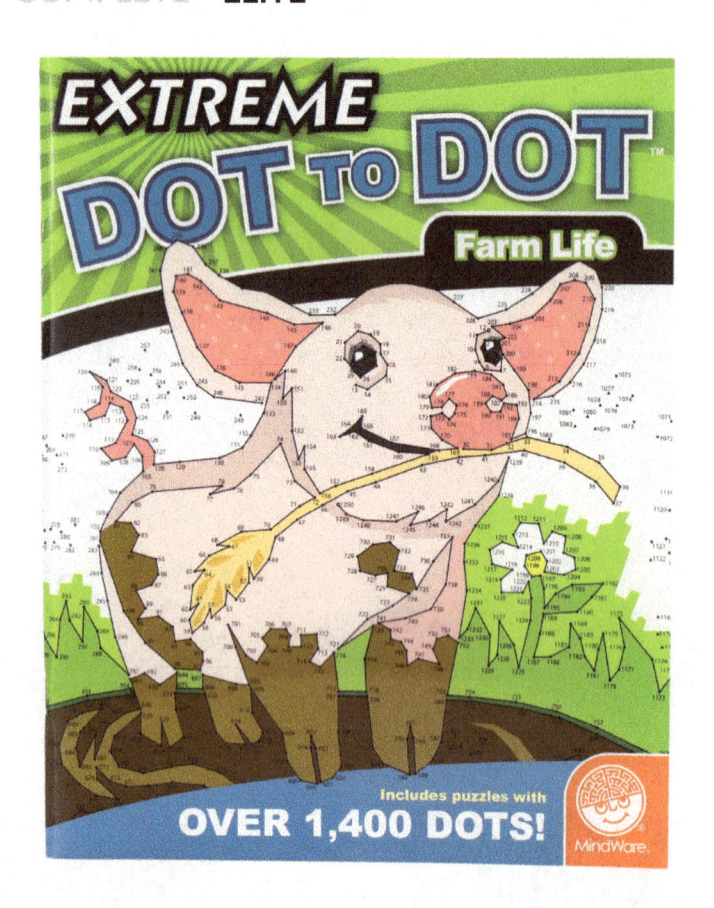

Kick-start your student's mental focus with the amazing Extreme Dot-to-Dot: Farm Life. Unlike conventional dot-to-dot puzzles that reveal too much of the picture and ruin the mystery, Extreme Dot-to-Dot: Farm Life puzzles are intricate and so challenging that when your student looks at a page, he will have no idea what the end result will be.

Mapping and concentration are just two of the educational benefits to solving these dot-to-dot puzzles. Both your student's left brain and right brain will be exercised as he works to complete puzzles containing 400 to over 1,400 dots. Some puzzles even cover a two-page spread, definitely not for the faint-hearted.

Enter the noisy world of the barnyard with Extreme Dot-to-Dot: Farm Life, which includes 32 puzzles of interesting farm creatures and scenes, such as pigs in the mud, a blue-ribbon cow, and 30 others!

Scheduling
With 32 puzzles in all, completing 1 a week will set a perfect pace.

THINKING SKILLS

THIS IS AS CRITICAL AS IT IS APPEALING

In Timberdoodle's curriculum kits, you will find a rigorous pursuit of thinking skills for every child, in every grade. This is simply not an optional skill for your child. A child who can think logically will be able to learn well and teach himself logically in ways that an untrained brain will find difficult.

Be thankful that you won't have to persuade your child to learn to think, though – he's wired for problem solving! We're guessing this portion of the curriculum will be the hardest not to race through. After all, who doesn't want to work through a thinking skills puzzle book, solve the mystery of the colorful balls, or be the first to snatch the golden die?

BUILDING THINKING SKILLS
COMPLETE ~ ELITE

Building Thinking Skills books are among our favorites because of their tremendous scope. Studies have shown that students using these books have raised their national test scores significantly in both content and cognitive tests!

Building Thinking Skills develops four basic analytical skills (similarities/differences, sequences, classification, and analogies) through both figural and verbal problems. In addition, there are problems dealing with deductive reasoning, map skills, Venn diagrams, mental manipulation of two-dimensional objects, and much more.

One thing to note is that some sections your child will likely blaze through, while others will require some time to reap the full benefits, particularly the sections regarding writing descriptions of objects. If these portions leave your student fainthearted, consider having him dictate every other page or type all his answers rather than writing them. Better yet, encourage him that these skills are ones he will really use, whether he's a pilot navigating his plane or a dad telling his toddler where to put his dirty sock.

Scheduling
Completing 10 pages a week will get you through the entire book in a year. Most children will love that pace, but if it is too much for your student, feel free to drop that back to four to five pages a week and work through it in two years.

ColorKu

COMPLETE ~ ELITE

Sudoku, the numbers game where players fill each of the blank boxes in a puzzle based on specific rules, has received a makeover. Introducing ColorKu, where the use of colors rather than traditional numbers makes ColorKu much more accessible to sudoku novices, children intimidated by numbers, or just lovers of beauty. ColorKu will improve your child's memory and logic, and it will require him to think strategically and solve problems creatively. The gorgeous wooden playing board is a generous 12" x 12" and comes with 81 wooden marbles in nine intense colors. The included dimpled-plastic tray pulls double duty as both a cover when ColorKu is not being used and as a ball holder while playing ColorKu.

Scheduling
Over 100 challenges are included, so we suggest doing 3 new challenges a week. On your last three weeks, convert any standard sudoku puzzle into a ColorKu by substituting one color for each number. Now you'll never run out of challenges!

ULTIMO
~~COMPLETE~~ ELITE

Easy to learn and fast to play, Ultimo is at its core pure mathematical stratagem ingeniously disguised as a simple game.

There are 15 dice in three groups. One die is gold. The object of the game is to get the gold die. Take 1, 2, or 3 dice each turn. The catch? You can't take the gold die until the last play of the game!

While the concept is straightforward, winning the game requires abstract strategy and the ability to do some forward-thinking, perfect for your students.

Suitable for two players and a wide age range, Ultimo is the ultimate strategy and probability game for the entire family. In light of that, don't limit yourself to just you and your child playing. Rope in another child, a grandparent, or even a shut-in at your local assisted-living facility.

Scheduling
Unlimited. We suggest breaking it out for a round or two at least once a week.

HISTORY & SOCIAL STUDIES

HOW DID COW FAT START A REVOLUTION?

Many history curriculum options make the mistake of starting with U.S.A. history. As important as that is, doesn't it make more sense to start with the big picture of history? This year you'll learn about the Modern Age, covering the major historical events in the years 1850–1994. You'll answer questions like:

- Where was the Crystal Palace?
- Who was the Sick Man of Europe?
- And, of course, how did cow fat start a revolution?

Geography this year will be equally intriguing as you play geography games and complete the vibrant pages of Skill Sharpeners Geography to master important geography concepts.

Many families have found that graphic novels provide huge incentives to their budding readers. The pictures will help your student to stay focused and make him want to understand the written text. With the True Stories of War and 24-Hour History sets of graphic novels, your student will be immersed in the places and times he's studying. What a way to bring those to life!

STORY OF THE WORLD
COMPLETE ~ ELITE

This is very easy to use. Just have your child read one section from the story book, then ask him to tell you what it was about. Afterwards, pick an activity page or worksheet that is appropriate for your child's interest and your schedule.

Did you see how big the activity book is? Keep in mind that one of the activity book's biggest advantages is the fact that it offers a wide range of activities for each lesson. Pick the ones that best fit your child's learning style and your family's schedule, but don't try to do them all!

One brilliant way to use this text is to approach it from a notebooking perspective. To do this, you'll want to grab your child a blank notebook that he will fill with his recap ("narration") of each chapter. As he goes, he'll add art, maps, and even photos of more tangible projects that he does. This is a somewhat labor intensive approach, but if you're eager for your child to have a firm grasp on world history, it is hard to beat this method for helping him retain what he learns.

Scheduling
Completing three chapters every two weeks is a realistic pace that will get you through the books in just under a year.

If you purchased the Elite kit, you'll love having the audio book. It includes the same content as the story book, but it can be much more convenient. Your child can just pop in the CD and listen to his history with as many of the rest of the family as would like to participate. What a treat!

Would you like to coordinate the graphic novels in your kit with your readings in Story of the World? Here's where to put them in:

True Stories of the Civil War: chapter 5
True Stories of WWI: chapters 20–21
True Stories of WWII: chapters 28–29
24-Hour History Pearl Harbor: chapter 28
24-Hour History D-Day: chapter 29
24-Hour History Apollo 11: chapter 35
24-Hour History John F. Kennedy: chapter 36
24-Hour History Martin Luther King Jr.: chapter 36

SKILL SHARPENERS GEOGRAPHY
COMPLETE ~ ELITE

Skill Sharpeners Geography lets your child explore his world while learning key map skills and geography concepts with little fuss on your part. The cross-curricular activities integrate the most current geography standards, and each eye-catching book is divided into colorful collections of engaging, grade-appropriate themes.

Each theme includes short nonfiction reading selections, comprehension questions, vocabulary practice, and writing prompts.

In this grade, each chapter has a rhythm to it. First, there are a couple of pages of reading, a few questions, and some visual literacy exercises—usually maps or the like. Next is a page of vocabulary practice, using fun things such as crosswords or word searches, etc. Then you'll find an involved, hands-on activity such as designing a passport or performing an archaeological dig. (This is an optional project; consider it extra credit!) Finally, you'll find a writing exercise. While the prompts are worthy, not every student needs this extra writing practice. If it's too much for your child, we suggest having him simply answer verbally or record his answers on your phone.

Skill Sharpeners Geography takes your child beyond just the basics of geography and includes a smattering of histories and cultures within our world. The colorful illustrations and pages will grab your child's attention, and the handy (removable) answer key in the back allows you to help your student easily check his work.

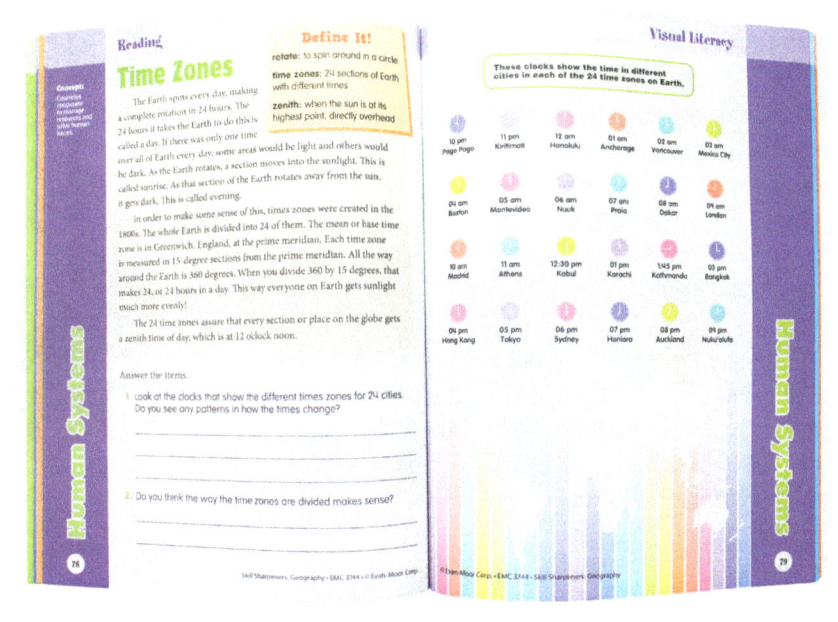

Scheduling

With 132 pages in all this year, simply complete 4 a week to stay on track. Add in the activities as time and interest allow.

And yes, you may truly skip the activity and writing pages (with no guilt) if that isn't how your child learns best.

True Stories of War

COMPLETE ~ ELITE

Many families have found that graphic novels provide huge incentives to their budding readers. The pictures will help your student to stay focused and make him want to understand the written text.

You'll be thrilled that he's not only enjoying reading, but that he's also getting a memorable, insightful look at history. Be forewarned, though, that war is far from pretty. However, this series does a tasteful job of showing what it would have been like to live through these events without depicting unnecessary gore.

In True Stories of the Civil War, he'll read the stories of the people who lived through it. From the first shots on Fort Sumter to the surrender at Appomattox, True Stories of the Civil War will give your child a visual look at the war that nearly tore our nation apart.

During World War I, known as the Great War, many soldiers kept journals about their experiences. True Stories of World War I encapsulates six of them, including Alvin York and the Red Baron. Your child will learn of the horror of gas warfare and the tragic sinking of the Lusitania.

Using the unique accounts taken from actual diaries and letters, True Stories of World War II tells the stories of five men and women who fought for their countries during World War II. From the Bataan Death March to the sinking of the USS Indianapolis, this graphic novel will open your child's eyes to the horrors of a war that must never be repeated.

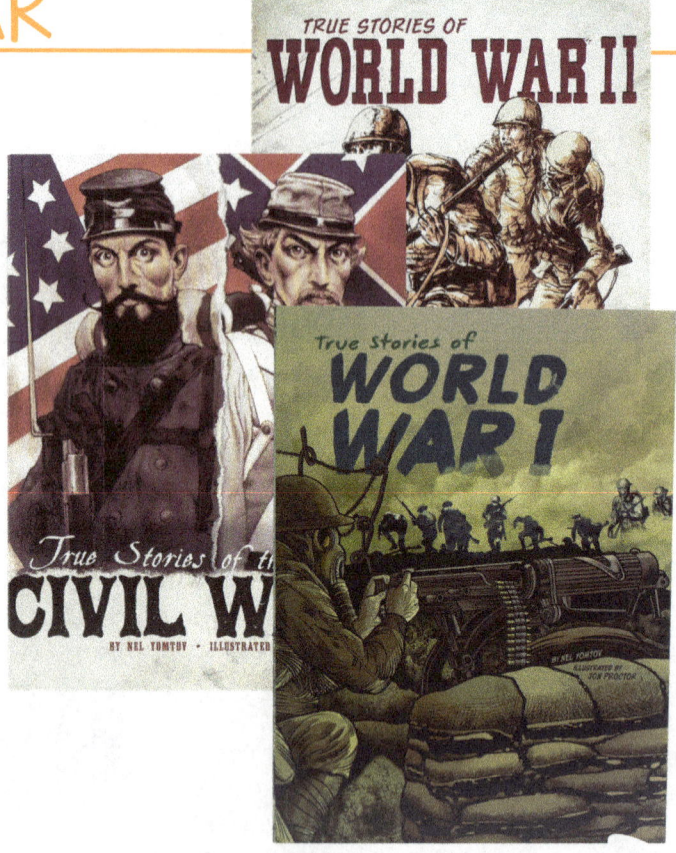

Scheduling

We suggest not assigning these books but just letting your student read them and see what he thinks. Or save them for when they tie into The Story of the World—if your student can leave them alone that long! (That would be in chapters 5, 20-21, and 28-29 of Story of the World, FYI.)

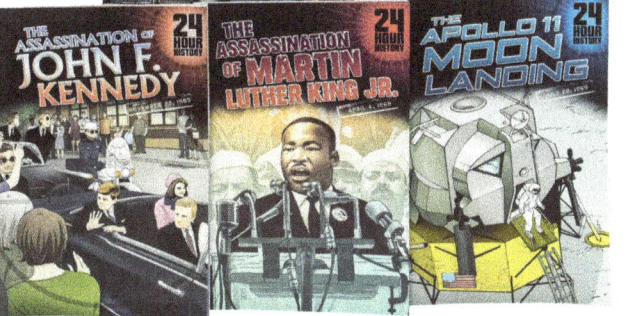

24-HOUR HISTORY

~~COMPLETE~~ **ELITE**

In each of the five 24-Hour History graphic novels, your child will learn key events that happened in a very short amount of time, but which still have impact today. At the back of each 24-Hour History book are short biographies of some of the key characters, timelines, pertinent maps or diagrams, and a glossary. 24-Hour History will provide your child with an action-packed introduction to key historical events.

Scheduling
Unlimited. You can spread out the fun by assigning one book every month or two, save these books for a dreary afternoon, use them where appropriate for Story of the World, or, perhaps best of all, hand them over to your child immediately so he can read and re-read them as often as he likes.

2020-2021 4th-Grade Nonreligious Curriculum Handbook • 800.478.0672

SCIENCE

LEARN ALL THE SCIENCE!

Because science disciplines are so interconnected, to learn one subject requires a foundational understanding of another. Building Blocks of Science addresses this by introducing students to the five core scientific disciplines of chemistry, biology, physics, geology, and astronomy.

Building Blocks of Science has 22 chapters, with 4 chapters about each of the five core science subjects, plus an introductory and a concluding chapter. With Building Blocks of Science, students learn science in a sequential and logical order, while hands-on experiments for each chapter encourage critical thinking, experimentation, and creativity.

Your student is also going to love the Dr. Bonyfide series! He'll study the bones of his feet, legs, and pelvis while having a blast with this captivating, colorful book.

DR. BONYFIDE 2
COMPLETE ~ ELITE

Dr. Bonyfide is a young person's highly entertaining guide to his own body. You know that if your child has basic information about his body he is more likely to make healthy life choices. Plus, isn't it natural to want to understand why your body works the way it does?

Developed by a team of educators, health professionals, and parents, Dr. Bonyfide Presents will creatively guide your child through the bone structures of his body using kid-friendly jokes, rhymes, puzzles, fun facts, and original comic strips. Plus, a pair of "X-ray vision" (colored) glasses will let your child investigate the bones on special pages. Write-in quizzes and a range of hands-on activities will help you as a teaching parent to assess his progress while simultaneously helping him retain his new knowledge.

Scheduling
With 112 pages in all, plan on doing 3–4 a week if you want to make this course last all year. But be prepared–your child may find it so engaging that he races through and finishes it early!

BUILDING BLOCKS OF SCIENCE
COMPLETE ~ ELITE

Because science disciplines are so interconnected, to learn one subject requires a foundational understanding of another. Building Blocks of Science addresses this by introducing students to the five core scientific disciplines of chemistry, biology, physics, geology, and astronomy.

Building Blocks of Science has 22 chapters, with 4 chapters about each of the five core science subjects, plus an introductory and a concluding chapter. With Building Blocks of Science, students learn science in a sequential and logical order, while hands-on experiments for each chapter encourage critical thinking, experimentation, and creativity.

Each chapter has five components, two of which are considered essential:

The lesson (essential - in the student textbook)
Experiment and record (essential - in the laboratory notebook)
Connections to Explore (in the digital lesson plans)
Self-review sheet (in the digital lesson plans)
Self-test or other exam (in the digital lesson plans)

FYI, the self-review sheet is basically a structured blank page to fill out with whatever your student remembers about the lesson, while the self-test is similar, but in a write-your-own-test format.

Digital Access
Your course includes access to some very unique digital files. (Didn't get the access info? Check your invoice or drop us a line and we'll get you squared away.)

First up is the lesson planner, with everything from a helpful overview of planning to printable stickers to use for scheduling your weekly lessons.

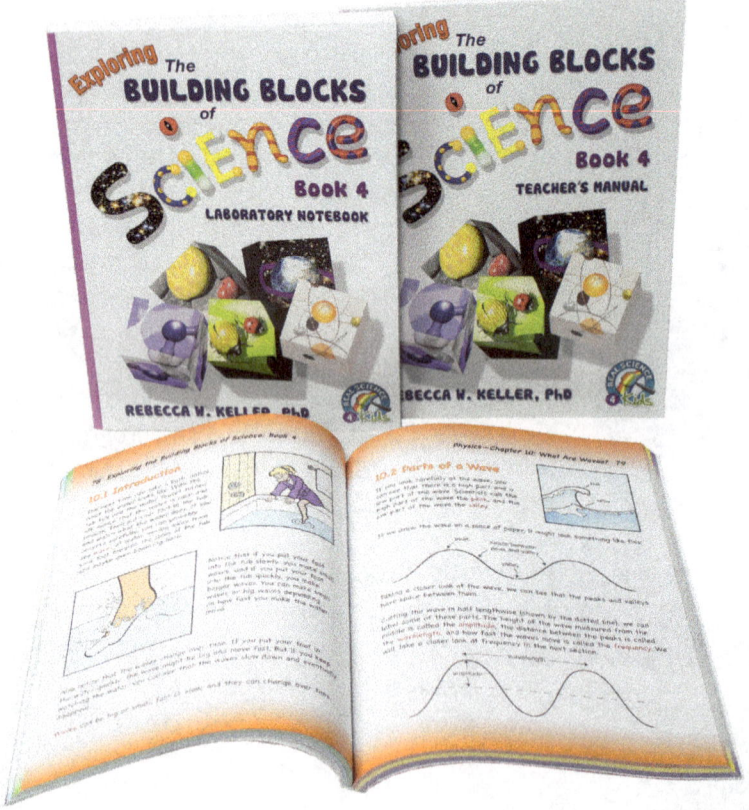

Secondly, you'll notice all of the optional testing materials. Use those if your child loves testing, your state requires it, or you're looking for opportunities to reinforce test-taking skills. Otherwise, feel free to set those aside.

Thirdly, take a look at the study notebook. This is different from the laboratory notebook included in your kit. It includes a ton of cut-and-paste, sort-and-file type activities. If your student loves art or you're in a state that requires so many hours of school, these are seriously wonderful activities. However, if these activities don't fit your schedule, don't worry. They are a beautiful supplement, but they are not essential.

Scheduling

You'll see that the publisher suggests completing one lesson a week. This is the easiest way to go, but there are only 22 lessons in all. Of course, you can choose to finish early, take some weeks off, or spread lessons out over two weeks, as desired.

Or, if you'd like a more precise formula, we'd suggest doing one part of a lesson each week:

Read the lesson
OR
Do the experiment(s) & complete the laboratory notebook

In a standard 36-week school year you'll need to combine both parts eight times. We suggest doing that on the first or last 8 weeks of school to make planning your schedule easy.

Pro Tip:

The most intimidating part of science can be gathering the supplies required for experiments. If you purchased the Elite kit, take advantage of the lab kit included. If not, we recommend you stop now, grab a box and the list of materials printed in the introductory pages of your textbook, and collect all your needed materials, purchasing any items you need for the year on your next shopping trip. Make it more fun by considering it a full-family scavenger hunt!

Besides everyday dishware and perishable items, you should be able to collect most other items you need, and you'll never regret having already completed the most labor-intensive step of your child's science education this year.

STEM LEARNING

STEM IS EVERYWHERE!

STEM learning is more than robotics and computer programming. STEM tools are those that engage students in exploratory learning, discovery, and problem solving, thus teaching the foundational skills of critical thinking, short-term planning and long-term planning. So STEM includes your Pixel Mosaics kit as well as your ColorKu logic game even those these are found elsewhere in this guide. Basically anything that goes beyond a rote read-and-regurgitate lesson undoubtedly falls into the STEM classification. In assembling this guide, many of our products could easily have been classified as STEM, but these components seem especially appropriate for this category.

ROBOTIS DREAM 2.0
COMPLETE ~ ELITE

Further your child's interest in science or construction with Robotis Dream's multiple configurations and solid documentation. This 12-week or 24-week curriculum comes with an easy-to-understand workbook(s) with clear pictures and text, plus thought-provoking questions that will guide your child through a simple introduction to robotics. He will also have the opportunity to design and build his own robots using a geared motor for independent movement—no programming required. Robotis Dream presents topics such as electricity, the center of gravity, the understanding of power, and the walking mechanisms of both two- and four-footed robots through lessons on science, technology, engineering, and math.

Scheduling
Each set has been designed as a 12-week course. If you get just Level 1 you could opt to complete 1/3 of a "week's work" every week to stretch the program out.

Or, if you received Levels 1 and 2, you are set up for 24 weeks of robotics. As in all of your work this year, feel free to blaze ahead if your student is ready for more!

MY CRAZY INVENTIONS SKETCHBOOK

COMPLETE ~ ELITE

Some years ago the top buzzword for business was "creative." A few years later, the hot topic in education became creativity.

This trickle-down development should spur educators, especially those of us teaching at home, to look beyond easy "read-and-regurgitate" education that dulls the mind. Instead, we should lead a lifestyle that not only encourages imaginative efforts, but that also passionately carves out time for those pursuits every day.

The finest method we have found is both surprisingly easy and affordable – doodle books. A doodle a day has the potential of engaging both sides of the brain and unleashing a powerhouse of originality. And, with so much variety, it never gets old.

Inventing is a characteristic of being human, yet surprisingly enough, in today's read-and-regurgitate academic climate, it is not something that is actively pursued. My Crazy Inventions Sketchbook: 50 Awesome Drawing Activities for Young Inventors can change that.

With its pages and pages of creative prompts, My Crazy Inventions will inspire brainstorming, imagining, and ultimately, drawing. Each spread contains numerous fun-filled illustrations of real and imaginary inventions and scenarios plus lots of room for your child's own inventive drawings. "Invent a brand-new candy, a writing tool your friends would like to use, or something that would help you sleep better at night."

My Crazy Inventions has illustrations of actual inventions, and it is bursting with fun facts of inventions that have succeeded (M&M's) and failed (a car wash for humans). My Crazy Inventions is beautifully crafted, with thick pages ready for multiple as your child fine-tunes his design. Also included is an application for a patent and a patent certificate, suitable for framing.

Scheduling

With 50 activities to complete, we suggest doing 1 or 2 a week. Enjoy!

Note: Some pages may not be suitable for all families, most notably a page with a bikini-clad sunbather.

STEM OR STEAM?

STEM, an acronym for Science, Technology, Engineering, and Mathematics, has recently been joined by Art to form STEAM. Is it really that important? Yes! Art is used to plan the layout of a tower, the design of a prosthetic hand, and the colors of the latest app. In fact, as long as your project is inquiry-based and you have the opportunity to think critically, creatively, and innovatively, then you are looking at a STEAM curriculum. Because the transition of terminology from STEM to STEAM is still tentative, we are using STEM for clarity's sake and listing art here separately in this handbook. But don't let that fool you into overlooking art this year. It really is a vital skill!

HEY CLAY ANIMALS
COMPLETE ~ ELITE

Hey Clay Animals is a clever fusion of spongy, stretchy modeling clay and an interactive animated app that will teach your child step by step how to make a herd of cheerful animals.

The brightly colored modeling clay is not sticky, yet the sculpted parts hold together well.

The Hey Clay Animals app will give your artist step-by-step directions on how to build the animals, from the selection of clay color to what type of shape to make and where to place it. These detailed, self-paced tutorials are all your child will need to produce professional looking models. Once his clay creation has air-dried, it is ready for display or play.

Hey Clay Animals encourages fine motor skills and spatial reasoning, and it will inspire your budding professional clay artist.

Clay is nontoxic, wheat- and gluten-free, and it won't stick to hands or stain other objects. However, the lovely texture doesn't emerge until after a few minutes of kneading. Some of our testers were disturbed by the initial texture and very relieved when a few minutes later it felt amazing!

Scheduling
There are six detailed animals to build. You'll want to allow enough time to complete an animal start-to-finish in a single sitting, as stopping in the middle can make the remaining pieces unable to stick well. (If you absolutely have to stop mid-animal, we suggest popping the assembled parts into a zip baggie to see if that will keep it from drying out before your child can get back to it.)

We suggest building one a month to spread out the fun, but if you think keeping the remaining dough airtight will be a challenge, why not do them all in a single week when your student is stuck indoors due to weather or illness?

Note:
During the air-drying process (about 24 hours), Hey Clay may leave a color residue on some surfaces. To avoid this, we recommend drying Hey Clay on a piece of plastic wrap, foil, white scrap paper, or another disposable surface.

DJECO AT NIGHT
COMPLETE ~ ELITE

Scratch art is a type of engraving where an artist scratches through dark ink to uncover a colored layer beneath. The French company Djeco has taken scratch art to a whole new level with these original, display-worthy designs.

Follow the directions and embellish parts of the creative scratch artboards with simple zentangle-like patterns. In other places, larger areas of the boards are scratched off to reveal hidden surprises. With the nighttime-themed Djeco At Night, your child will scratch away the surface to uncover exquisite glow-in-the dark nightlife designs.

Djeco At Night includes four cards featuring glow-in-the-dark nightlife designs, one scratch tool, and a full-color instruction booklet filled with inspiring design ideas. Djeco At Night will boost both your child's fine motor and visual discernment skills.

Scheduling
This kit includes 4 artboards, each of which will take some time to complete. We suggest working on one at least 15 minutes a week for the best result, or complete them one at a time during weeks with more free time than normal.

Pro Tip
Your student may find it easiest to work with a clean paper or mat underneath his scratch art to catch crumbs and something like a piece of paper or cloth to wipe the stick on.

DJECO KHAN MOSAICS
~~COMPLETE~~ **ELITE**

This beautiful art-by-numbers kit, Khan Mosaics, creates two impressively illustrated pictures any preteen would enjoy. By just following the numbers and adding the correctly colored foam sticker tile to the backgrounds, he will assemble two imposing pictures: a grumpy gorilla and a thoughtful tiger. The vibrant Khan Mosaics is a small, quiet, easy-to-pack activity to tuck into a purse for traveling, be it to the local homeschool meet-up or around the world. Lots of fun with virtually no mess, Khan Mosaics will keep your child engaged and entertained for hours. What a pleasant way to exercise and strengthen hand-eye coordination, fine motor skills, and concentration.

Scheduling
There are just two mosaics, yet each will take a fair bit of time to finish. Whittle away at it every week until completion or save this kit for a long plane trip, a family gathering where the adults need quiet, or the 2021 Snowmageddon!

WRITE AND DRAW YOUR OWN COMICS

~~COMPLETE~~ **ELITE**

Learn how to create characters, think up story ideas, write dialogue, use sound effects, draw action, and convey emotions with Write and Draw Your Own Comics.

Creating comics is not only one of the best ways to encourage creative writing, but because comics don't have to be funny, they can also be used to recount a history lesson, illustrate a science principle, or explain current events.

Using simple step-by-step instructions, practical tips, and handy hints, this exciting activity book will show your child how to create imaginative graphic stories. The spiral-bound "lay-flat" presentation is full of brilliant advice, and this book even includes over 130 cartoon-style stickers for your child to add to his creations.

For the child who loves to tell stories but favors graphics over words, Write and Draw Your Own Comics will help develop skills that may prove to be useful for a lifetime.

Scheduling
With 95 pages in all (including the introductory matter), we suggest your child completes about 3 pages a week. Or have him complete one of the 24 chapters a week and anticipate finishing early. You could ask your child to use the remaining 12 weeks to turn in a weekly comic strip/story of his choosing.

Pixel Mosaics

~~Basic~~ ~~Complete~~ **ELITE**

At the end of the 19th century, painters used a technique called pointillism, a technique in which small, distinct dots of color are applied in patterns to form an image. With Pixel Mosaics, paints and brushes are replaced with pegs, and the end result is stunning.

Choose from dozens of different images of animals, great works of art, landmarks, landscapes, famous people, even Star Wars characters, and print the pattern cards. With just six different colors, your child's Pixel Mosaics creation will look like it was made of thousands of colors and tones when viewed from a distance. It makes an elegant wall hanging for your living room or a fun decoration for his bedroom.

And, when you want a change, just dump the pegs back into the box, choose another Pixel Mosaics template, and create something new. Pixel Mosaics includes four connectable peg boards; 6,800 pegs; and one picture frame.

Pro Tips:
At the time of this printing, there are 129 mosaic patterns on their website for free downloading. Of those, about 50 would require either extra individual colors (we do stock those if you're interested) or some thoughtful modifications. Of course, there are dozens and dozens of patterns that require no additional pieces, but you'll want to check that before you get started to save frustration.

When you go to print your chosen design, you will want to print the PDF on plain paper with Adobe Acrobat set to "actual size" (i.e., exactly the same as the perforated board), rather than "fit to page" which may shrink them, making them unusable.

Scheduling
This set truly is unlimited. We suggest planning to have your child spend at least 20 minutes a week on it and see how many masterpieces he can create this year.

LEARNING TOOLS

HOW DOES YOUR CHILD LEARN BEST?

Do you know your child's learning style? If not, you should take a few moments to research it. Once you know your child's strengths and weaknesses, you'll be able to focus on methods that actually help him learn instead of simply using the approach you've always used. (All learners usually find it helpful to integrate as many learning modes as possible into their studies.)

For instance, if you find you have a kinesthetic learner, allow and encourage him to move while he learns. Break out the Thinking Putty, let him sign keywords to himself, or write them on a whiteboard. If he's an auditory learner, make it a point to have him hear the information he's learning. You could read it to him, encourage him to read aloud, use an audio version, or download a podcast, but however you decide to approach it, he will be much better off than simply reading and re-reading the same textbook silently four dozen times. By the way, visual learners will probably find that they have the easiest time learning – after all, most information is naturally presented visually in any textbook.

MIXED BY ME THINKING PUTTY
COMPLETE ~ ELITE

If you've been around Timberdoodle for long, you already know about our passion for Thinking Putty and the difference it can make for a fidgety student.

This kit takes that tool to a whole new level by encouraging your student to name and develop his very own custom putty. Want a little guidance? Try one of these ideas:

Name It First
Have him come up with an idea first, then build the putty to suit. Perhaps he will want a putty that reminds him of scuba diving with Uncle Tim. Or perhaps he'd like to perfectly match the color of that gorgeous sunrise.

It's a Theme!
He could name (or even develop) all five of the putties around a single theme. For instance, would you say the two completed ones shown on the previous page are jade and copper? Or are they perhaps seaweed and crab?

Pro Tip
These tiny putties really only need a pinch of colors or special effects. As tempting as it will be to put in all of it, he may want to use only 1/5th of any add-in for a single tin until he has decided for sure that he doesn't want any of that add-in for the other four tins!

Scheduling
Plan to make up at least one Thinking Putty in the first week of school. Completed putties are perfect for playing with while he watches his math lessons or at other times when his mind is more engaged than his hands.

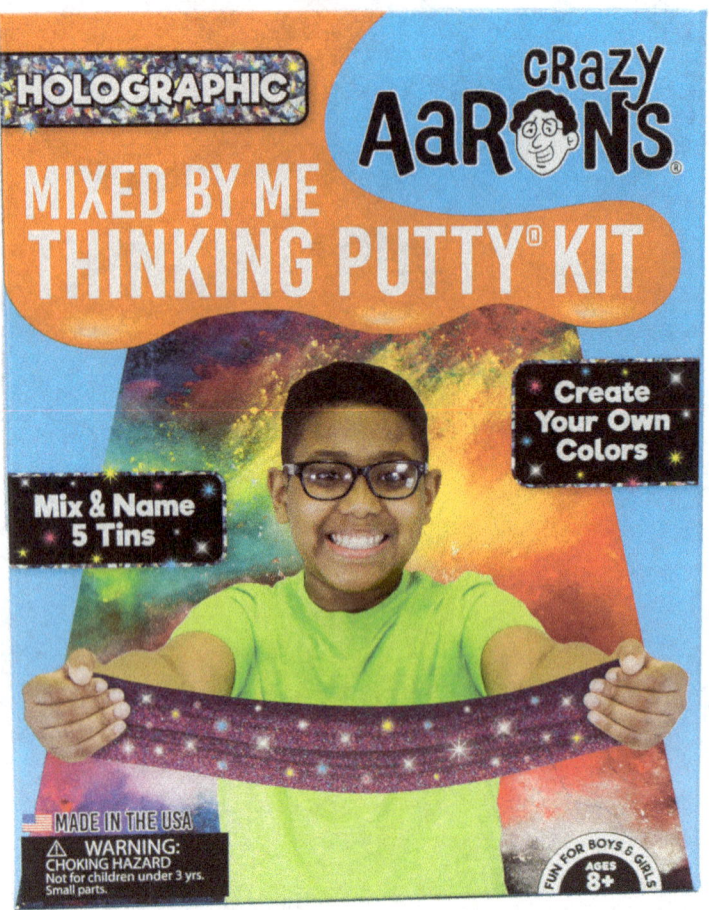

TEST PREP
COMPLETE ~ ELITE

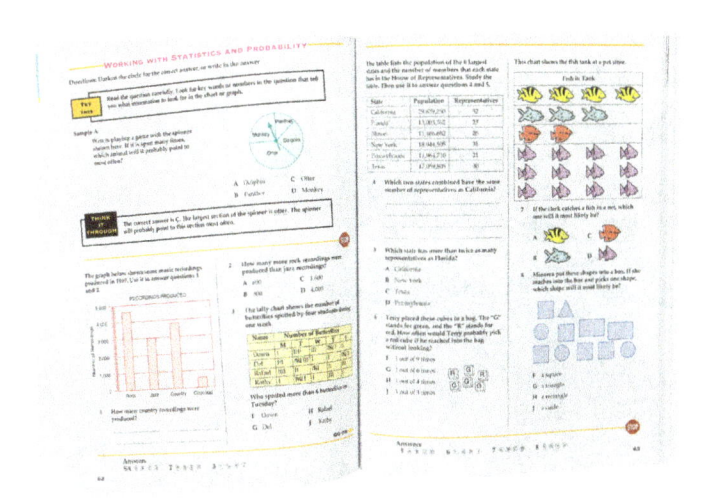

Home-taught children who are not prepared for their yearly standardized tests are at a distinct disadvantage to the government- and privately-taught children. If you reside in a state that requires standardized tests, you should know that a vast majority of certified teachers teach with the test in mind. In other words, teachers understand the types of questions that will appear on the standardized tests, and they will spend weeks preceding the tests covering the necessary information. If you do not do likewise, your children stand a chance of performing poorly in comparison.

For those of us in a state where some form of testing is required, but never scrutinized, preparing is not as critical. But some of you are in states where the test results are not only analyzed but are used as a basis for whether you may continue to home educate. Why not make sure your children are "playing on a level playing field"? The Test Prep series offers students the essential groundwork needed to prepare for standardized tests.

Based on subject areas covered by most state standardized tests, these colorful, inviting workbooks provide a good sampling of all the skills required of each grade level. Practice pages, strategies, tips, and full-length practice tests build test-taking confidence and skills in subjects such as reading comprehension, vocabulary, language, and math. The test tips are beneficial, and the information and instructions are super-easy to follow. Developed by a leading educational publisher, Harcourt's Test Prep provides a great opportunity for children to review before taking standardized state tests. Engaging, practical, and easy to use, Test Prep will help your children face the tests with the same confidence that their peers will have.

Even if your state doesn't require testing, consider completing the book anyway, since test-taking skills are vital across all areas of life.

Scheduling
Our family has always preferred to spend the week or two before our state-mandated annual testing working through this book. Keep it low key, and let the change of pace be an enjoyable experience for your child. If you run into a concept he doesn't know, stop and explain it to him; that is why you are doing the prep now!

68

THE ARTICLES

FROM OUR FAMILY TO YOURS

In 1986, we were a family of five. I was the oldest of three toddler girls with a mom who absolutely excelled at educating us at home. Of course, this was during "The Dark Ages" of homeschooling, and online searching was still a thing of the future. Our mom, Deb, was (and is) a voracious reader, though, and an avid researcher. We girls were thriving academically and, naturally, other moms were interested in using the same curricula Deb had found.

So, in 1986 she and Dan, our dad, repurposed the business license originally intended for their world-class Golden Retriever breeding operation (which had come to naught), and she launched Timberdoodle, a homeschool supply company. A catalog was born, and growth came fast. We shipped from our laundry room, the grandparents' basement, and finally, warehouses and an office. Two more children were added, and all of us grew up working in the business from an early age.

Now, decades later, Timberdoodle is still renowned for out-of-the-box learning and crazy-smart finds. Mom's engineering background has heavily influenced our STEM selections, and her no-nonsense, independent approach has made these kits the award-winning choice that they are today.

All five of us are grown now, and most still work at Timberdoodle in key roles. Our brother and his wife have welcomed sweet new babies, and we sisters have opened our home to children through foster care and adoption. As our families have grown, we've become even more committed to equipping parents with the best homeschooling resources. The kits we sell are the same ones we use in our own homes, and we hope you enjoy them as much as we do.

In the following articles, you'll hear from Deb and others about some of the nitty-gritty questions we often field. Do you have a question not answered here? Don't forget that you are invited to contact us at any time—we'd love to help!

Joy (for all of us)

WHAT MAKES GAMES A PRIORITY?

6 REASONS GAMES AREN'T JUST FOR FUN, EVEN THE "FRIVOLOUS" GAMES

You may have noticed that this year there is at least one multi-player game in every curriculum kit. This is not just to add some levity to your day!

The Research
A quick google search will net you numbers of articles on the benefits of playing board games iwith your children. Here are just some of those benefits:

- increasing laughter
- language development
- understanding rules
- grasping fair play
- detecting patterns and predicting outcomes
- learning from experience
- impulse control
- social skills
- increasing focus
- teamwork
- reducing anxiety
- unplugging from technology
- increasing analytical abilities
- setting goals
- patience
- problem solving skills
- reducing stress
- creativity
- prioritizing steps towards a goal
- self-confidence
- spatial ability

This is a robust and interwoven list, but here are the five things that have jumped out at us over the past year and made this a huge priority for your child's education.

1. Social-Emotional Intelligence
Think of your closest and dearest friends outside of your immediate family. What makes them so dear to you? My guess is that it isn't their IQ or ability to speed-solve a complex math problems. A friendship will celebrate those interesting facts, but your friendship itself is more likely rooted in shared interests, time spent, and an ability to navigate hard situations with grace.

When you spend time teaching a child how to lose graciously, you are teaching a life skill that will translate into all of life and impact their friendships way more than their test scores ever could.

In light of this the end of each game may be more important than the strategy in the middle. Coach your children in what you expect from the winner and the loser. Around here, a "Good game!" goes a long way, but you decide what is best for your family. Humility is what you're looking to see. Not the teary deflation of a proud loser or the puffed up bragging of a proud winner!

2. Strategic Thinking
Obviously, the games we've chosen require age-appropriate logic and strategy. Critical thinking skills are essential, so let's teach them any way we may.

3. Connection
It can seem that as your children get older your parenting gets more and more hands-off. Or, for a younger child, it may seem that you spend more time correcting behaviour than you do connecting with your child. Making games a priority lets you enjoy each other's company and genuinely become closer to each other. What parent won't appreciate that?

4. Executive Functioning
Are you familiar with executive functioning? It is the ability to prioritize and organize information. The clearest example we've been given is the age old challenge to "guess what number I'm thinking of right now using yes or no questions." If you respond by asking if the number is higher than 100, you are using executive functioning. If instead you start rattling off numbers, you're not. In games you're constantly taking into consideration what your opponent is doing, what pieces are still in your hand, which rules apply at the moment... and sorting/utilizing all the information to decide what your next game play should be.

5. Regulation
Some articles tie this to executive fuctioning, but it's worth discussing on its own. Regulation is the ability to control your own emotions - can you think of a more natural opportunity to practice this than during game play? Calm-down strategies and redos may be implemented as many times as needed, until your child is able to endure suspense and even win or lose without outbursts. Phew!

6. Growth Mindset
Yes, this is a buzzword right now, but it is worth mentioning. Some of us, students included, tend to think that we are good at something or we're not. For our PreK twins this has been particularly obvious in our discussions about art. One has a natural inclination for drawing and one does not. So the naturally gifted one calls himself an artist and proclaims that his brother is not. It is helpful to come back and discuss that we all learn and grow. So when Mr. Artist set aside his art for several months and his twin worked and worked at it, we had two artists on our hands! Gameplay is a natural place to model that all of us learn and grow in our skill sets. You aren't simply "born with it" but you learn skills and develop abilities.

Side Note: Think Out Loud
An article from Parenting Science made an excellent point that student's don't always naturally ask why a player used a specific strategy. Try to start that conversation by asking why he chose to _ or explain that you're starting with this piece because _. This will model the higher order thinking that you are setting out to teach. It will also model the fact that we are all learners here!

So what are you waiting for? Go play some games!

WHY EMPHASIZE INDEPENDENT LEARNING?

THE TOP SEVEN REASONS THIS IS SUCH A BIG DEAL AT TIMBERDOODLE

1. Avoid Burn Out
One-on-one teaching is critical to the success of any student, and homeschoolers are no exception to that. However, we have seen parents who become helicopter teachers, micromanaging every detail of their students' education. Is it any wonder that these parents burn out? Independent learning tools provide a natural transition from the one-on-one of early childhood to a less teacher-intense educational approach.

2. Cultivate Responsible Learners
There is a lot of (dare we say it?) fun in teaching. But it is better for your students if they master how to learn on their own. After all, when they are adults, you'll want them to have the ability to pick up any skill they want and learn it as needed. Structuring their education to be more and more self-taught helps them to become responsible self-learners.

3. Special Needs, Illness, and Newborns
Not all parents have the same amount of teaching time. Whether they are doing therapy for a child with autism, dealing with their own chronic illness, managing visits for a foster child, or are blessed with a newborn, there are seasons when homeschooling needs to be more independent simply for the teacher's sanity!

4. You Don't Have to Love Teaching
As much as no one wants to mention this, we all know parents who really struggle to teach. They love their kids and feel strongly about homeschooling, but

when it actually comes down to teaching, they are easily overwhelmed and intimidated. If it is an area they are not gifted/trained in, then of course teaching, is scary. Independent learning tools can help get them comfortable in their role, but even if they never love teaching they can still reap the benefits of giving their children a superior education at home.

5. Timberdoodle's Purpose: We Are Here to Make Giving Your Children a Superior Education at Home Enjoyable

Here at Timberdoodle, amid the catalogs, sales, blog posts, videos, Facebook giveaways, etc., we have one primary goal. That goal is to make it possible for parents to enjoy giving their children a superior education at home. We aren't here to sell you stuff (though we wouldn't exist if you didn't shop!), which is why we have been known to send you to our "competitors" when their product would work better for you. We really just want you to be a happy homeschool family. When that happens, we feel successful! Independent learning is one tool in your toolbox. It is a valuable tool, so use it where it works best for you.

6. Not Either/Or

You don't have to pick between independent and group learning across the board. Take The Fallacy Detective, for instance. It is designed for a student to pick up and read independently. Instead, our family did it as a read-aloud and took turns answering the questions. The result? Not only did we have a blast, but we were also all on the same page regarding logical fallacies. Bumper stickers and ads we came across in daily life were fodder for vigorous discussions about the underlying fallacies in ways that would never have happened if we each studied it alone. So even if you're striving to teach independent learning, don't hesitate to do some things together!

7. Our Family

The rule of thumb in our house was that as soon as a child could read, he or she was responsible for his or her own education. We each had an annual conference with Mom to set learning goals for the year, then we were given the books for the year, often including the teacher's manuals. Mom gave us each a weekly checklist to complete before Friday Family Night. If we needed help, we were to ask for it. Otherwise, the responsibility was ours. This freed us up to do the truly important things (service, Timberdoodle work, babysitting, elder care, community projects, hospitality, farming...) as a family.

9 Reasons to Stop School Work and Go Build Something!

Would you like to supplement your curriculum with a program that simultaneously improves your child's visual perception, fine motor skills, patience, problem solving, spatial perception, creativity, ability to follow directions, grasp of physics concepts, and engineering ability? Better yet, what if your child would actually enjoy this curriculum and choose to do it whenever he could? No, this isn't some mythical homeschool product guaranteed to solve all your problems for a large fee—we are talking about the LEGO® bricks already strewn throughout your house, the blocks in our preschool curriculum, and the Bioloid robot kit designed for teens.

Construction kits just might be the most underrated type of curriculum ever. It's not just us; research concludes that children learn a lot by designing and building things. Based on our own engineering background/bias, we believe that construction is one of the most valuable educational processes available, for that reason, both learning to build and learning by what has been built should be a part of every family's curriculum. Here are our top nine skills your child will learn with his construction kit:

1. Visual Perception
It may be obvious that it takes visual perception to find the right pieces and place them well, but consider that whether your child is reading, finishing a puzzle, or doing open-heart surgery, a proficiency in visual perception is mandatory!

2. Fine Motor Skills
Boys especially seem to struggle with fine motor skills, particularly when it comes to writing and drawing. Amazingly enough, though, they are often the most passionate about building—the natural remedy! The more they fine-tune their dexterity, the easier "school time" becomes for both of you!

3. Patience
Do you know anyone who couldn't stand to be a little more patient? Construction takes time. Slowing down, reading the directions, doing it over when a piece has been placed wrong or a sibling knocks over your creation… these are all valuable character-building experiences!

4. Problem Solving
Some children simply lack the ability to troubleshoot a situation and figure out the next step. Construction sets provide a structured opportunity to figure out what went wrong and fix it, if you're following the directions. If you are designing your own models, you'll have even more opportunities to problem solve!

5. Spatial Perception
Probably the clearest picture of how important it is to be able to mentally convert 2D images into 3D objects is that of a surgeon. Knowing where the spleen is on a 2D textbook page isn't nearly the same thing as being able to reach into an incision and find the damaged spleen!

6. Creativity
Not every creative person has artistic ability. But construction can open the doors of creativity like no other tool. What if I move this gear over here? Could I build that bridge with only blue pieces?

7. Following Directions
Some children are natural rule followers and need to be encouraged to be creative. Others need to constrain themselves to follow directions, at least on occasion! If your child falls into that camp, construction kits are a natural way to encourage him in this skill, with the added benefit of a finished result he can show off!

8. Grasp of Physics
Friction, force, mass, and energy are all basic physics concepts much more easily explained and grasped with a set of blocks and a ball than simply by studying a dry textbook definition!

9. Engineering Ability
Many "born engineers" are not drawn to textbooks. But set a construction kit in front of them and watch them explore pulleys, levers, wheels, and gears. They'll soon go from exploration to innovation, and you'll be amazed at their inventions!

WHAT IF THIS IS TOO HARD?
9 STEPS TO TAKE IF YOU'RE FEELING OVERWHELMED

Everyone has felt overwhelmed at some point in his or her education. Whether it's a groan from you as you pull a giant textbook out of the box or the despair from your child when he's read the directions five times and the robot STILL isn't operating as he wants it to, you will almost certainly hit a moment this year when you realize that an aspect of homeschooling is harder than you anticipated.

So, what do you do now?

1. Take a Breath
Just knowing that everyone faces this should help you relax a bit. This feeling will not last–you'll get through this!

2. Jump In!
Why are you stressed right now? Are you stressed because "it" is so intimidating that you haven't been quite ready to dive into it? If that's the case, the simplest solution is to jump in and get started. Could you read the first page together before lunch? What if you have your student find all of the pieces for step one today? Sometimes it's better to muddle through a lesson together than to wait until you're ready to teach it perfectly.

3. Step Back
Perhaps you're too close right now. If you're mid-project with incredible effort and totally frustrated by how it's going, try the opposite approach. Close the book for 30 minutes (set a timer!) and go grab lunch, hit the playground, or swap to a more hands-on project. When the timer rings, you and your student will be ready to try again with clearer heads.

4. Time This
Timers are an invaluable learning tool. If you're being distracted, try setting a 10- or 20-minute timer during which you'll do only _____. Or tell yourself you definitely need to tackle That Dreaded Subject, but only for 30 minutes a day, in two 15-minute chunks. When the timer rings, close the text and move to the next thing. Dividing your day into blocks of time can make a remarkable difference in your efficiency level.

5. Level Down
Did your student take the math placement test before jumping in this year? Perhaps he is just in the wrong level! If moving to an easier level kind of freaks you out, it may help to remember that you and your student are not defined by his skill set in any field, and faking his way through by blood, sweat, and tears does not help his future self. Taking the time to back up and fill in the gaps, though, will benefit him forever!

6. Simplify
If you are trying to do every possible activity in every course, it's no wonder you're exhausted. By the time your student is in high school, he will need to complete 75% or more of the work in each course to get full credits. We're not advocates of doing the work in name only, but it's okay to watch some experiments online rather than completing each one in the

dining room. It's also appropriate to only do every other math problem in a section if your child is bored to tears with yet another page of addition. Doesn't that feel better?

7. Make Accommodations
What exactly is stressing your student (or you!) out right now? Is it the pen-to-paper writing component? Why not let him use the computer and type his work instead? Or perhaps he can dictate to you while you write for him. Make sure you're doing whatever you can to engage his best learning style. Encourage Mr. Auditory Learner to read aloud if necessary. Or break out all of the favorite fidgets and let Miss Kinesthetic work at a standing desk.

8. Get Help
Ask another teacher/parent to take some time working through the issue with you. You may be surprised by how much clarity you gain with a fresh set of eyes. (Our Facebook groups can be great for this!)

9. Get Professional Help
Check the publisher's website, the book's teacher page, or the kit's manual for contact information. Most of the authors and manufacturers we work with are fantastic about helping and coaching those who get stuck. Not getting the help you need from them? Contact mail@Timberdoodle.com or call us at 800-478-0672, and we'll work with them to get that answer for you.

9 Tips for Homeschooling Gifted Children

1. Disdain Busywork

Your child wants to learn, so don't slow him down! If he has mastered multiplication, why are you still spending an hour a day reviewing it? Yes, he does need some review, but we've seen way too many families focus on completing every problem rather than mastering the material. One way to test this is to have him try doing only every other review problem and see how he does. If he can prove he's mastered it, he doesn't need to be spending quite as much time on it.

2. Go Deep

Allow breathing room in your schedule so you have time to investigate earth's gravitational pull or the advantages/disadvantages of hair sheep vs. woolly sheep. Remember that your child is asking to learn, so why pull him away from the subject that's fascinating him? After all, we all know that material we're interested in sticks with us so much better than things we learn only because we must.

3. Go Fast

If your child wants to take three science courses this year or race through two math levels, then why not let him? Homeschoolers can absolutely rock this because there are no peers holding them to a "traditional" pace!

4. Encourage Completion

Sometimes I think there is a touch of ADD in every genius. Give your child as much flexibility as you possibly can, but also keep in mind that you'll be doing him a disservice if he never has to tackle something he doesn't feel like working on at the moment. Sometimes he may even be surprised to realize that the very subject he dreaded is the springboard for a whole new area of investigation!

5. Give Space & Opportunities

If you can keep mandatory studies to a minimum, you'll give your child more opportunities to accelerate his learning in the areas he's gifted at. Common sense, perhaps, but also worth deliberately thinking through as you plan out your school year.

6. Work on Weak Areas Carefully
While you definitely want to work with him to help him overcome areas he's just not as strong in, you also want to be careful that a weakness in one area doesn't impede his progress in other ways. For instance, a child may struggle with writing simply because his brain works much faster than his hands. While I encourage such a family to work on handwriting skills, I also suggest that they try teaching their child to type and allow him to complete writing assignments on the computer. This lets him continue to build his writing skills instead of holding him back because of his lack of handwriting speed.

7. Emphasize Humility & Service
We have met way too many children who are obnoxiously convinced that they are geniuses and that everyone needs to be in awe of their abilities. Your child will be much healthier (and happier!) if he realizes these four things:

- His identity is NEVER found in his brainpower.

- Even as gifted as he is, there are still things that others do better than he does.

- He is much more than his brain. (Should he lose his "edge", he won't lose his worth!)

- His gifts are not for himself alone, but even more important, they are for him to use in serving.

Of course, the goal is never to insult or degrade him but to give him a framework from which he can truly thrive and be free to learn. With a proper perspective, he'll be able to enjoy learning without the burden of constantly assessing his genius and worrying what people will think of him. Don't weigh him down by constantly telling him how big his brain is, either. Encourage his learning, but don't forget to cultivate his character at all costs. In 10 years, his response to rebuke will be much more telling than his test score this year, so don't put an inordinate stress on intellectual pursuits.

8. Talk a LOT!
Talk about what he's interested in. Talk about the theories he came up with today. Talk about his daydreams. Talk about what he wants to study up on. Talk about why he may actually need to master that most-dreadful-of-subjects, whatever that may be to him… Not only will you be able to impart your years of wisdom to him, but you'll also know well the subjects he's interested in and be able to tie those in to his other studies, the places you're visiting next week, or that interesting article you read yesterday.

9. Relax!
Your child is a wonderful gift; don't feel that every moment must be spent maximizing his potential. As a side benefit, just relaxing about his genius may in fact increase it. Our own family found that some of our best test scores came after a year off of most formal schooling! Not what we would have planned, but a very valuable insight. Living life=learning, so maximize that!

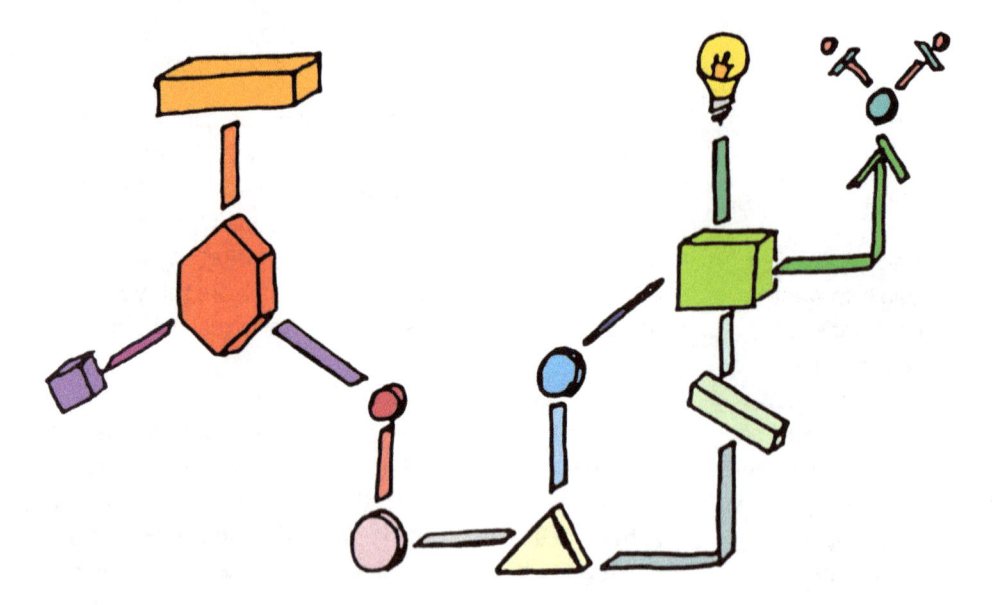

Convergent & Divergent Thinking

Have you considered the necessity of incorporating both convergent and divergent thinking into your learning time? Experts recognize these as the two major types of brain challenges we all encounter.

Does that just sound like a whole bunch of big words? No worries, let's break it down. Your child needs to be able to find the right answer when needed (math, medicine dosage) and also needs to be able to come up with a creative, unscripted answer when the situation warrants (art, architecture...).

A child who can only find the "right" answer will be a rigid thinker who can't problem-solve well or think outside the box.

A child who only thinks creatively will not be able to follow procedures or do anything that involves math.

What Is Convergent Thinking?
To go more in-depth, convergent thinking generally involves finding a single best answer and is important in the study of math and science. Convergent thinking is the backbone of the majority of curricula and is crucial for future engineers, doctors, and even parents. Much of daily life is a series of determining right and wrong answers, and standardized tests favor the convergent thinker. But when we pursue only convergent-rich curricula, we miss the equally vital arena of divergent thinking.

Is Divergent Thinking Different?
Yes! Divergent thinking encourages your child's mind to explore many possible solutions, maybe even ideas that aren't necessarily apparent at first. It is in use when he discovers that there is more than one way to build a bridge with blocks, to animate a movie, or even simply to complete a doodle. Radically different from read-and-regurgitate

textbooks, divergent activities are not only intellectually stimulating, but kids love them, too.

Make a Conscious Effort to Include Both in Your Curriculum

Admittedly, because most textbooks and even puzzles are designed for convergent thinking, you will need to make a conscious effort to expose your children to multiple opportunities for divergent thinking. It is imperative because both divergent and convergent thinking are necessary for critical thinking to be effective.

Why Doctors Need Both Skills

As an example, let's look at a medical doctor. A physician needs to be extraordinarily skilled at convergent thinking to dose medications correctly, diagnose life-threatening emergencies, and follow safety procedures to avoid infection. However, the first person to wash his hands before surgery or to find a treatment for Ebola used divergent thinking. Some of the best doctors today are those who employ powerful convergent skills to accurately diagnose, paired with curiosity and divergent thinking to find the most effective or previously undiscovered treatment plans.

Convergent in Fourth Grade

From reading to math, the backbone of your curriculum this year is convergent. This makes sense, because so much of learning at this level is simply marveling at facts. Sometimes there really is a right answer!

Divergent in Fourth Grade

These tools include strong divergent aspects to help your child become a well-rounded thinker:

- **My Crazy Inventions Sketchbook**
- **Write and Draw Your Own Comics**
- **Robotis Dream**
- **Ultimo**

Robotis actually teaches both convergent and divergent thinking. When your child is recreating the robots as instructed, that's a convergent skill. But when he creates his own versions that's divergent thinking!

Similarly, games like Ultimo use convergent rules and logic, but because of the dynamic nature of gameplay there are many instances of divergent thinking throughout the game.

HELP! MY BOOK SAYS "COMMON CORE"!

THE TRUTH ABOUT WHETHER YOUR TIMBERDOODLE CURRICULUM KIT IS ALIGNED WITH COMMON CORE

There's been a lot of buzz, discussion, and anxiety in the homeschool community for the last decade about the Common Core State Standards. Many of you have asked us what our stance is on the standards and whether our curriculum is designed to comply with them.

What Is the Common Core?

According to the CCSS website, "The Common Core State Standards Initiative is a state-led effort that established a single set of clear educational standards for kindergarten through 12th grade in English language arts and mathematics that states voluntarily adopt."

But Isn't That a Good Idea?

Growing up as an Air Force "brat," Deb, Timberdoodle's founder, attended many different schools throughout her educational career. She can tell you just how much easier it would have been for her if all of the schools covered the same materials in the same order. Then, she could transfer effortlessly between them instead of missing critical information because the new school had already covered something her old school hadn't addressed yet. So, yes, the concept may be brilliant, but there are some very valid concerns.

Why Homeschoolers Are Concerned

There is some real concern in the homeschooling community about what the Common Core Standards Initiative will mean to our families. In an early article posted by the Homeschool Legal Defense Association, HSLDA Director of Federal Relations William Estrada wrote, "The CCSS specifically do not apply to private or homeschools… However, HSLDA has serious concerns with the rush to adopt the CCSS. HSLDA has fought national education standards for the past two decades. Why? National standards lead to national curriculum and national tests, and subsequent pressure on homeschool students to be taught from the same curricula."

Declining Quality?
Some in the homeschooling community have also expressed concern that as curriculum publishers endeavor to align with the CCSS, the educational quality in those texts will actually decrease rather than improve, while some are disenchanted with the atypical teaching methods employed by the CCSS, among other concerns.

What We Are Doing
At Timberdoodle, our approach is simple. We are ignoring the CCSS and continuing to search out crazy-smart curricula, exactly what we've been doing for the past 30+ years. Our specialty has always been hand-picking the best products in every subject area and offering the families who trust us the same products we have used or would happily use ourselves. And we have no plans to change the way we carefully review every resource we sell.

Some Products Do Say Common Core
Some of the items in this kit do, in fact, align with the CCSS. Not because we've sought that out, but because the quality resources we've chosen for our curricula are already up to that standard or beyond. It is no surprise to us that the excellent tools we are excited about are also good enough to exceed the qualifications for the CCSS.

This Has Never Changed and Will Not Change Now
At Timberdoodle, we work with trusted publishers and products we review carefully, not just in math and language arts but in all subject areas, so that we feel confident we are providing some of the best resources available for your children. Every time an item we've loved is revised (or stamped Common Core), we make sure that it has not been watered down or made confusing. Our goal is to exceed educational requirements, not by aligning our curriculum with any government standard, but by continuing to find products that work well and meet the high standards we hold for our families and yours.

Mosdos Ruby Weekly Assignments

A SAMPLE DETAILED SCHEDULE

Here's one way to break down your assignments to flow easily through a 36-week schedule.

The page numbers refer to the current student reader as of this printing.

You'll notice that some weeks have more titles assigned than others. We've taken into account the number of corresponding workbook pages and the length of the readings to come up with these weekly assignments, but you should always feel free to rearrange in whatever fashion works for you. The surrounding content (e.g. introductory matter or sidebars) varies too, and your mathematically inclined student will quickly notice that no two weeks have identical page counts. Remind him that this is a good time to learn how to be flexible and persistent. After all, he may even find that the longer stories end up being his favorites!

Please note that you only need to complete as many of the corresponding activity pages and assignments as you determine to be appropriate for your reader. Our family would have chosen to answer the Studying the Selection questions in the readers orally rather than in writing. We would also likely skip the writing assignments since you'll be covering writing systematically with Daily 6-Trait Writing.

SUGGESTED WEEK-BY-WEEK PLAN
UNIT 1
The Things That Matter

WEEK 1
Lesson in Literature... What Is a Story? — page 2
Leah's Pony — page 4
The Way — page 16
Jill's Journal: On Assignment from the Dirty Thirties — page 18
Activity pages and assignments.

WEEK 2
Lesson in Literature...
    What Is Plot? — page 22
Supergrandpa — page 24
If You Think You Are
    Beaten — page 36
Activity pages and
    assignments.

WEEK 3
Lesson in Literature... Characters — page 38
Two Big Bears — page 40
March Bear — page 51
Jill's Journal: On Assignment in China — page 53
Activity pages and assignments.

WEEK 4
Lesson in Literature... What Is Setting? — page 56
Mom's Best Friend — page 58
Activity pages and assignments.

WEEK 5
Lesson in Literature... What Is Theme? — page 70
The Tiger, the Persimmon, and the Rabbit's Tail — page 72
Here She Is — page 84
Unit 1 Wrap-up — page 86
Activity pages and assignments.

UNIT 2
Clarity

WEEK 6
Lesson in Literature... What Is Internal Conflict? — page 92
Sato and the Elephants — page 94
Purple Snake — page 108
Activity pages and assignments.

WEEK 7
Lesson in Literature... What Is External Conflict? — page 110
Amelia's Road — page 112
Since Hanna Moved Away — page 122
Jill's Journal: On Assignment in the Supermarket and the
    Field — page 124
Activity pages and assignments.

WEEK 8
Lesson in Literature... What Is Sequence? — page 128
The Hatmaker's Sign — page 130
Activity pages and assignments.

WEEK 9
Lesson in Literature... What Is Foreshadowing? — page 144
Dad, Jackie, and Me — page 146
Analysis of Baseball — page 158
Activity pages and assignments.

MOSDOS RUBY WEEKLY ASSIGNMENTS CONTINUED, WEEKS 10-24

WEEK 10
Lesson in Literature… What Is a Main Idea? — page 160
And Now the Good News — page 162
Hurt No Living Thing — page 173
Jill's Journal: "They Loaded Up Their Trunks and They Moved to Tennessee" — page 175
Unit 2 Wrap-up — page 180
Activity pages and assignments.

UNIT 3
Head, Hands, Heart

WEEK 11
Lesson in Literature… Characters — page 186
Eddie, Incorporated — page 188
Jill's Journal: On Assignment at the Town Dump — page 209
Activity pages and assignments.

WEEK 12
Lesson in Literature… Major and Minor Characters — page 212
Heatwave! — page 214
Be Glad Your Nose Is on Your Face — page 228
Activity pages and assignments.

WEEK 13
Lesson in Literature… What Is Dialogue? — page 230
The Wright Brothers — page 232
The Inventor Thinks Up Helicopters — page 244
Jill's Journal: On Assignment in Dayton, Ohio — page 246
Activity pages and assignments.

WEEK 14
Lesson in Literature… What Is Internal Dialogue? — page 250
The Imperfect/Perfect Book Report — page 252
You and I — page 264
Activity pages and assignments.

WEEK 15
Lesson in Literature… Point of View — page 266
Justin Lebo — page 268
Holding Up the Sky: A Tale from China — page 278
Unit 3 Wrap-up — page 280
Activity pages and assignments.

POETRY
These weeks have no workbook pages. Enjoy the break!

WEEK 16
Bird's Square Dance — page 288
Thistles — page 289
Whirligig Beetles — page 290

This Is the Key — page 291
Any assignments.

WEEK 17
A Bridge Engineer — page 294
A Bugler Named Dougal MacDougal — page 294
A Funny Young Fellow Named Perkins — page 295
A Native of Chalamazug — page 295
A Gullible Rancher Named Clyde — page 295
Any assignments.

WEEK 18
Seasons Haiku — page 298
A Seeing Poem — page 302
Popsicle — page 303
Any assignments.

WEEK 19
The Shark — page 306
Dust of Snow — page 307
Any assignments.

WEEK 20
Some Opposites — page 310
Tortillas Like Africa — page 311
Any assignments.

WEEK 21
Good Hotdogs — page 314
Jackrabbit — page 316
Any assignments.

UNIT 4
Caring

WEEK 22
Lesson in Literature… Creating a Setting — page 324
Earthquake Terror — page 326
Michael Is Afraid of the Storm — page 343
   Jill's Journal: On Assignment in New Madrid — page 345
Activity pages and assignments.

WEEK 23
Lesson in Literature… What Is Imagery? — page 348
The Gift — page 350
For You — page 364
Activity pages and assignments.

WEEK 24
Lesson in Literature… Comparing Settings — page 366
Toto — page 368
In This Jungle — page 382
Activity pages and assignments.

MOSDOS RUBY WEEKLY ASSIGNMENTS CONTINUED, WEEKS 25-36

WEEK 25
Lesson in Literature... What Is Mood? — page 384
Owl Moon — page 386
Activity pages and assignments.

WEEK 26
Lesson in Literature... What Is Biography? — page 398
Homeward the Arrow's Flight — page 400
Jill's Journal: On Assignment in Britain to Speak with the Lady with the Lamp — page 415
Unit 4 Wrap-up — page 420
Activity pages and assignments.

UNIT 5
Determination

WEEK 27
Lesson in Literature... Author's Purpose — page 426
Underwater Rescue — page 428
Today the Dolphins Came to Play — page 442
Jill's Journal: On Assignment Exploring the Mesoamerican Reef — page 444
Activity pages and assignments.

WEEK 28
Lesson in Literature... What Is Stated Theme? — page 446
The Seven Children — page 448
Activity pages and assignments.

WEEK 29
Lesson in Literature... What Is Implied Theme? — page 460
The Garden of Happiness — page 462
Johnny Appleseed — page 475
Jill's Journal: On Assignment in Crista's Garden — page 477
Activity pages and assignments.

WEEK 30
Lesson in Literature... Drawing Conclusions — page 480
One Grain of Rice — page 482
Activity pages and assignments.

WEEK 31
Lesson in Literature... Compare and Contrast — page 498
Maria's House — page 500
City I Love — page 518
Unit 5 Wrap-up — page 520
Activity pages and assignments.

UNIT 6
The Grand Finalé

WEEK 32
Lesson in Literature... Elements of Fiction — page 526
The Bridge Dancers — page 528
Activity pages and assignments.

WEEK 33
Lesson in Literature... Elements of Nonfiction — page 542
Dancing Bees — page 544
Activity pages and assignments.

WEEK 34
Lesson in Literature... Elements of Drama — page 550
Name This American — page 552
Activity pages and assignments.

WEEK 35
Lesson in Literature... Fictionalized Biography — page 568
Boss of the Plains — page 570
Activity pages and assignments.

WEEK 36
Lesson in Literature... Pulling It All Together — page 584
Stone Fox — page 586
Unit 6 Wrap-up — page 602
Activity pages and assignments.

Now celebrate! You've made your way through a very rich year's study of literature!

549 Book Suggestions

So you love the idea of the reading challenge, but you'd like a boost to get you started? You've come to the right place!

Customize This!
You'll find a few ideas here for each challenge, but don't forget that you're not bound to our list. There are literally hundreds more options that may be even better for your family. Use these pages as starter ideas and not as your final list.

Will I See the Same Books Over and Over?
No, not on this list! However, you can expect to see some of these books appear on the lists for more than one grade (so if you have a third-grader and a fourth-grader, some parts of the list will match), since books are often appropriate for more than one grade level.

Many books could easily fit into more than one category, but we only put each in one place on your list for your convenience. (Books that are part of a series are the one exception, as you may find an individual title in one spot and the whole series referenced elsewhere.) So if you're finding that you want to read more than one book from a particular challenge, the odds are good that skimming the list will give you another challenge to list it under. For instance, *Heidi*, from challenge 10 (a book more than 100 years old), would also fit really well under challenge 12 (a book about relationships or friendship), challenge 45 (a book about a girl), or challenge 88 (a book set in Europe). Shuffle things as you like!

Repeated Authors

In this grade you'll find a lot of Boxcar Children, Trixie Belden, Happy Hollisters, etc. Not a fan? Just skip them! But most kids love the repetition of finding the same heroes in a new story, so we have not hesitated to include much of the series throughout the challenges when appropriate.

A Variety of Reading Levels

Some of these books are clearly geared as a read-aloud at this age and would be challenging for most fourth-graders to read independently. However, most of the books do fall into the range of material typically suggested for a fourth-grader. Our suggestion would be not to worry much about which books are read by your student vs. yourself. Grab the titles that interest you and him, and then flip through them. Which is he ready to enjoy reading? Set those aside for him. The rest you'll read to him. As your year progresses and his skills increase, you'll likely find you are setting more and more books aside for him to read. Read-alouds meet your child's tremendous need for literacy, language, and stories, though, so never shy away from simply reading to him!

A Note About Our Book Ideas

If you've been reading to your child long (or if you've simply perused your local public library), you've probably noticed that families have very different standards for their reading materials. The books you'll find listed here are ones that members of our team have read, have added to their "I want to read this" list, or have had recommended to them.

Even among our team there is a wide range in what titles our families would find acceptable. We've opted to include titles with abandon, knowing that you will be able to flip through them at the library to determine if they are a good fit for your family.

So this is not a "Timberdoodle would sell these books if we could" list. We can't vouch for each of the titles, and we certainly can't know which ones are a good fit for your particular family. Mostly we're providing this list to give you some ideas, just in case you're drawing a blank in thinking of books for a particular topic. Use these ideas as the jumping-off point for which they are intended, and, as always, we highly recommend previewing the books yourself.

Use Your Library

We can't overemphasize how useful your local library will be to you this year. We've listed multiple options under each challenge to try to ensure at least one title will be available. Now that most libraries allow you to place books on hold online, you'll find that you can use any spare hour in your day to request books for the next challenges and then whoever is in town next can swing by the library and pick them up. If you've not yet become a dedicated library user, this is the year!

549 BOOK SUGGESTIONS, CONT.

Reading and Talking

If you're newer to reading together, our biggest tips for you are these. First, just read together. Whether you read a page or read a book, you are making memories and building literacy. Don't overthink this—just squeeze it in as you can and watch reading time quickly become a highlight of your day.

Secondly, make sure you're discussing what you're reading. This doesn't need to be a formal book report on every book you encounter (please no!) or a tedious question and answer session every evening. Instead, talk as you go:

"Look at their faces! How do they feel? Why?"
"Do you like his choice? What would you do?"
"What do you think will happen next?"
"It looks like he thinks he is the most important. What's the truth?"
"What was your favorite part of this book?"

With these simple questions you are building emotional intelligence, worldview, logic, observational skills, and so much more.

Reading and Racism

It is worth noting that many of the books we grew up on have terrible racist undertones. (E.G. the neighbor in Little House on the Prairie who announces that "The only good Indian is a dead Indian," or those Tintin titles which portray people of color in negative ways.) We have kept some of these titles on our reading list because racism is a critical issue to discuss thoughtfully with your child, rather than just pretending it doesn't exist.

As our friend Tasha at Happy Homeschool Nest says:

What Can You Do: Teaching Your Family To Be Anti-Racist

Being anti-racist requires intentional and continuous action on your part as a mom. You set the tone for your home. Your children see what you truly value and believe. Waiting for "the right time" or when your child is "old enough" will be too late.

1. **Point out racism in movies and literature.** Classics especially. Think Little House on the Prairie for a minute. Dr Seuss. To Kill a Mockingbird. Adventures of Huckleberry Finn. I am not saying don't have these books on your shelves, but I am saying read them with your child and discuss why the author depicted the People of Color in those negative or rude ways.

2. **Discuss Hard Stuff.** You should always be explicit with children, of all ages, that racism is very hurtful and always wrong. Teach your child to be an ally. Teach them to speak up when they hear someone saying racist comments or jokes. Teach them to be a friend to the refugees, the low-income kids, the disabled kids, the Hispanic kids, etc etc.

3. **Diversify your shelves.** Find books and movies about People of Color, preferably where the storyline isn't about diversity. Continuously expose your child to the beauty and richness of the world--the peoples, cultures, religions, buildings, fashions and foods. Watch the hard things. Read hard books. Don't shy away from the hard conversations.

4. **Don't make racist jokes.** Period. Racist jokes are so hurtful because they are basically saying "you are so far beneath me, I can both conceal and express my prejudice and you can't do anything about it because it's socially acceptable —it's "only" a joke."

Looking for more on this subject? Her entire post on *How to Teach Anti-Racism and Why* is phenomenal. (We've quoted Tasha here with her permission.) Find her whole post here:

https://happyhomeschoolnest.com/blog/how-to-teach-anti-racism-and-why

Make This List Even Better

We love your book recommendations and feedback! Did you find a book you loved this year? We'd love to add your recommendations! Just shoot us a note at books@timberdoodle.com and let us know. Or were you perhaps disenchanted with one of our suggestions? Please let us know!

At the end of the year, fill out the Reader Awards on page 111 and submit that. We'll be thrilled to credit you 50 Doodle Dollar Reward points (worth $2.50 off your next order) as our thank you for taking the time to share.

549 BOOK SUGGESTIONS, CONT.

1. AN INSPIRATIONAL BOOK
The Children's Book of Virtues by William J. Bennett
The Children's Book of Heroes by William J. Bennett
Chicken Soup for the Kid's Soul by Jack Canfield
Real Kids, Real Stories, Real Change by Garth Sundem

2. A BOOK ABOUT THE WORLD
This Is the World by Miroslav Šašek
DK Pocket Genius: Earth
DK Eyewitness: Wonders of the World
If the World Were a Village by David J. Smith
DK Where on Earth? Atlas
The Usborne Encyclopedia of Planet Earth

3. A BIOGRAPHY
Harriet Tubman: Conductor on the Underground Railroad by Ann Petry
Who Was? series
Freedom Train by Dorothy Sterling
I, Galileo by Bonnie Christensen
To Fly: The Story of the Wright Brothers by Wendie Old
Meet George Washington by Joan Heilbroner
Meet Thomas Jefferson by Marvin Barrett
Meet Abraham Lincoln by Barbara Cary

4. A CLASSIC NOVEL/STORY
Little House series by Laura Ingalls Wilder
The Jungle Book by Rudyard Kipling
Betsy-Tacy series by Maud Hart Lovelace
The Wind in the Willows by Kenneth Grahame
The Swiss Family Robinson by Johann David Wyss
The Voyages of Doctor Dolittle by Hugh Lofting
The Chronicles of Narnia by C.S. Lewis

5. A BOOK YOUR GRANDPARENT (OR OTHER RELATIVE) SAYS WAS HIS/HER FAVORITE AT YOUR AGE
Ask your grandparents or relatives. Or, if that's not possible, ask your Facebook friends for a recommendation for your child.

6. A BOOK ABOUT ANCIENT HISTORY
The Story of the World: Ancient Times by Susan Wise Bauer
Who Was King Tut? by Roberta Edwards
Where Is Stonehenge? by True Kelley
Where Are the Great Pyramids? by Dorothy and Thomas Hoobler

7. A BOOK ABOUT SOMETHING THAT MAKES YOU HAPPY
What does your child treasure these days? If he's a budding coin collector, this is the perfect time to read a book on that. More of the run-around-outside type? How about a book on adventures? Hiking, tea parties, babies, grandparents... nothing is off the table for this story!

8. A BOOK BASED ON A TRUE STORY
January's Sparrow by Patricia Polacco
Pocahontas and the Strangers by Clyde Robert Bulla
Call of the Klondike by David Meissner and Kim Richardson
Bud and Me by Alta Abernathy
The Courage of Sarah Noble by Alice Dalgliesh
Keep the Lights Burning, Abbie by Peter and Connie Roop

9. A BOOK A PERSON AT LEAST TWICE YOUR AGE RECOMMENDS
Ask an older friend. He or she will likely be thrilled to recommend a book to you.

10. A BOOK MORE THAN 100 YEARS OLD
Heidi by Johanna Spyri
The Secret Garden by Frances Hodgson Burnett
A Little Princess by Frances Hodgson Burnett
The Wonderful Wizard of Oz by L. Frank Baum
Understood Betsy by Dorothy Canfield Fisher
Pollyanna by Eleanor Porter
Rebecca of Sunnybrook Farm by Kate Douglas Wiggin

11. A BOOK ABOUT FAMILIES
The Magnificent Mya Tibbs: Mya in the Middle by Crystal Allen
Gone Crazy in Alabama by Rita Williams-Garcia
The Vanderbeekers to the Rescue by Karina Yan Glaser
Five Little Peppers and How They Grew by Margaret Sidney
The Vanderbeekers of 141st Street by Karina Yan Glaser

Melendy Quartet books by Elizabeth Enright
The Littles series by John Peterson
Miracles on Maple Hill by Virginia Sorensen
All-of-a-Kind Family by Sydney Taylor
Sarah, Plain and Tall by Patricia MacLachlan

12. A BOOK ABOUT RELATIONSHIPS OR FRIENDSHIP
The Cricket in Times Square by George Selden
Jake Drake series by Andrew Clements
Friendship According to Humphrey by Betty G. Birney

13. A BOOK FEATURING SOMEONE OF A DIFFERENT ETHNICITY THAN YOU
Heart and Soul by Kadir Nelson
The Birchbark House by Louise Erdrich
Island of the Blue Dolphins by Scott O'Dell
Anna Wang series by Andrea Cheng
Wagon Wheels by Barbara Brenner
Om-kas-toe of the Blackfeet by Kenneth Thomasma

549 BOOK SUGGESTIONS, CONT.

14. A BOOK ABOUT SOMEONE WHO CAME FROM ANOTHER COUNTRY
Front Desk by Kelly Yang
Naming Liberty by Jane Yolen
Molly's Pilgrim by Barbara Cohen
Lily's Crossing by Patricia Reilly Giff
One Green Apple by Eve Bunting
A Journey to the New World by Kathryn Lasky

15. A BOOK OF FAIRY TALES OR FOLK TALES (OR AN EXTENDED RETELLING OF ONE)
African Folk Tales by Hugh Vernon-Jackson
The Classic Treasury of Hans Christian Andersen
The Candlewick Book of Fairy Tales
Grimm's Fairy Tales
The King's Equal by Katherine Paterson
The Ordinary Princess by M.M. Kaye
Fairy Tale Comics by Chris Duffy

16. A BOOK RECOMMENDED BY A PARENT OR SIBLING
Encourage your child to ask his parents or siblings for a book recommendation. Or, if he prefers to choose his own titles, have him ask for a couple of options from each and let him pick from that list.

17. A BOOK ABOUT THE OCEAN
Solving the Puzzle Under the Sea by Robert Burleigh
Oceans by Peter Benoit
Life in the Oceans by Lucy Baker
Dolphin Adventure by Wayne Grover
By the Great Horn Spoon! by Sid Fleischman
The Ocean Book by Frank Sherwin

18. A CALDECOTT, NEWBERY, OR GEISEL AWARD WINNER
Daughter of the Mountains by Louise Rankin
The One and Only Ivan by Katherine Applegate
The Tale of Despereaux by Kate diCamillo
Joyful Noise by Paul Fleischman
So You Want to Be President? by Judith St. George
Miss Hickory by Carolyn Sherwin Bailey

19. A BOOK ABOUT A HOLIDAY
The Best Christmas Pageant Ever by Barbara Robinson
A Charlie Brown Christmas by Charles M. Schulz
The Family Under the Bridge by Natalie Savage Carlson
Christmas in the Trenches by John McCutcheon
Christmas After All by Kathryn Lasky
When Christmas Comes Again by Beth Seidel Levine

20. A BOOK ABOUT GRANDPARENTS OR SENIOR CITIZENS
A Year Down Yonder by Richard Peck
How to Take Your Grandmother to the Museum by Lois Wyse and Molly Rose Goldman
The Last Best Days of Summer by Valerie Hobbs
The War with Grandpa by Robert Kimmel Smith
In Grandma's Attic by Arleta Richardson
When Grandmama Sings by Margaree King Mitchell
Grandfather's Dance by Patricia MacLachlan

21. A BOOK OF PUZZLES
The Puzzling World of Winston Breen by Eric Berlin
The Mysterious Benedict Society series by Trenton Lee Stewart
The Westing Game by Ellen Raskin
C D C? by William Steig

22. A BOOK THAT HAS A FRUIT IN ITS TITLE
Giant Pumpkin Suite by Melanie Heuiser Hill
Strawberry Girl by Lois Lenski
On the Banks of Plum Creek by Laura Ingalls Wilder
James and the Giant Peach by Roald Dahl
Little Pear by Eleanor Frances Lattimore

23. A BOOK ABOUT A FARM
Farmer Boy by Laura Ingalls Wilder
McBroom's Wonderful One-Acre Farm by Sid Fleischman
Moo by Sharon Creech
Babe: The Gallant Pig by Dick King-Smith
The Clippity-Cloppity Carnival **by Valerie Tripp**
Welcome to Silver Street Farm by Nicola Davies
A Farm of Her Own by Natalie Kinsey-Warnock
Corn Farm Boy by Lois Lenski

24. A BOOK ABOUT ILLNESS OR MEDICINE
Sadako and the Thousand Paper Cranes by Eleanor Coerr
Penny from Heaven by Jennifer L. Holm
The Lemonade Club by Patricia Polacco
A Doctor Like Papa by Natalie Kinsey-Warnock
DK Pocket Genius: Human Body
If I Die Before I Wake by Jean Little
Hero Over Here by Kathleen Kudlinski

25. A BOOK ABOUT SCHOOL, A TEACHER, OR LEARNING
Steamboat School by Deborah Hopkinson
The Magnificent Mya Tibbs: Spirit Week Showdown by Crystal Allen
Viking Adventure by Clyde Robert Bulla
Save Me a Seat by Sarah Weeks and Gita Varadarajan
The Wheel on the School by Meindert DeJong
The Year of Miss Agnes by Kirkpatrick Hill
Skippack School by Marguerite De Angeli
School Days According to Humphrey by Betty G. Birney
Who Was Booker T. Washington? by James Buckley, Jr.
Prairie School by Lois Lenski
Room One by Andrew Clements

26. A GRAPHIC NOVEL
Hereville: How Mirka Got Her Sword by Barry Deutsch
Bone series by Jeff Smith
Geronimo Stilton series
Babymouse series by Jennifer Holm
Disasters in History set from Graphic Library
Lost Trail by Donn Fendler
Or check our website for other series we love!

549 BOOK SUGGESTIONS, CONT.

27. A BOOK OF POETRY
A Light in the Attic by Shel Silverstein
The Llama Who Had No Pajama by Mary Ann Hoberman
Favorite Poems of Childhood by Philip Smith
The Oxford Illustrated Book of American Children's Poems
Julie Andrews' Collection of Poems, Songs, and Lullabies
Poems to Learn by Heart by Caroline Kennedy
Poetry for Young People series

28. A BOOK WITH A GREAT COVER
Let your child choose–it will be interesting to see what he considers to be a great cover!

29. A BOOK ABOUT FOOD
The Chocolate Touch by Patrick Skene Catling
The Candymakers by Wendy Mass
Stick Dog by Tom Watson
Food and Nutrition for Every Kid by Janice VanCleave
Adventures with Waffles by Maria Parr
Who Was Julia Child? by Geoff Edgers and Carlene Hempel
Fun with Food by Christy Webster
Cooking on the Lewis and Clark Expedition by Mary Gunderson
Cooking the Vietnamese Way by Chi Nguyen and Judy Monroe
Cooking the Israeli Way by Josephine Bacon

30. A BOOK ABOUT WEATHER
The Littles and the Big Storm by John Peterson
The Rainstorm Brainstorm by Valerie Tripp
Max Axiom Natural Disasters graphic novels
The Man Who Named the Clouds by Julie Hanna and Joan Holub
DK Eyewitness: Weather
DK Eyewitness: Hurricane & Tornado
Pink Snow and Other Weird Weather by Jennifer Dussling
What Was Hurricane Katrina? by Robin Koontz
Flood Friday by Lois Lenski
Explorers: Weather by Deborah Chancellor

31. A BOOK ABOUT AN ADVENTURE
The Worst-Case Scenario Ultimate Adventure: Everest by Bill Doyle and David Borgenicht
Jasper and the Riddle of Riley's Mine by Caroline Starr Rose
The Adventures of a South Pole Pig by Chris Kurtz
Lost on a Mountain in Maine by Donn Fendler
The Bears on Hemlock Mountain by Alice Dalgliesh
The Seven Wonders of Sassafras Springs by Betty G. Birney
Spy Mice series by Heather Vogel Frederick

32. A BOOK BY OR ABOUT WILLIAM SHAKESPEARE
A Stage Full of Shakespeare Stories by Angela McAllister
Graphic Shakespeare
Bard of Avon by Diane Stanley
Will's Words by Jane Sutcliffe
Usborne Illustrated Stories from Shakespeare

Shakespeare's Stories for Young Readers by E. Nesbit
The Shakespeare Stealer by Gary Blackwood
DK Eyewitness: Shakespeare
Tales from Shakespeare by Marcia Williams

33. A FUNNY BOOK
Hank the Cowdog series by John R. Erickson
Pippi Longstocking by Astrid Lindgren
Mr. Popper's Penguins by Richard and Florence Atwater
Mrs. Piggle-Wiggle series by Betty MacDonald
Knock-Knock Jokes for Kids by Rob Elliott

34. A MYSTERY OR DETECTIVE STORY
The Boxcar Children series by Gertrude Chandler Warner
The Happy Hollisters series by Jerry West
The Bobbsey Twins series by Laura Lee Hope
Trixie Belden series by Julie Campbell or Kathryn Kenny
Sherlock Jones series by Ed Dunlop
Nancy Drew series by Carolyn Keene
The Hardy Boys series by Franklin W. Dixon
The Crime-Solving Cousins series by Shannon L. Brown

35. A PICTURE BOOK
Choose one of your favorite picture books to re-read, or choose one you've never read before that appeals to you.

36. A BOOK BY OR ABOUT A FAMOUS AMERICAN
Rutherford B., Who Was He?: Poems About Our Presidents by Marilyn Singer
Our Country's Presidents by Ann Bausum
Childhood of Famous Americans series
Mr. Revere and I by Robert Lawson
Ben and Me by Robert Lawson
DK Eyewitness: First Ladies
Dk Eyewitness: Presidents

37. A BOOK ABOUT WESTWARD EXPANSION
Sacagawea's Strength by Stacia Deutsch and Rhody Cohon
The Secret Valley by Clyde Robert Bulla
The Quilt Walk by Sandra Dallas
The Sign of the Beaver by Elizabeth George Speare
Bound for Oregon by Jean Van Leeuwen
Only the Names Remain by Alex W. Bealer
Caddie Woodlawn by Carol Ryrie Brink
Tucket's Travels by Gary Paulsen
Tree of Freedom by Rebecca Caudill
If You Were a Kid on the Oregon Trail by Josh Gregory

38. A BOOK ABOUT 20TH-CENTURY HISTORY
A Place to Land by Barry Wittenstein
The Whispering Town by Jennifer Elvgren
Red Berries, White Clouds, Blue Sky by Sandra Dallas
24-Hour History set
The Titanic: Lost and Found by Judy Donnelly
Dorothea's Eyes by Barb Rosenstock
What Was the Holocaust? by Gail Herman
What Was D-Day? by Patricia Brennan Demuth
What Was Pearl Harbor? by Patricia Brennan Demuth
What Was the March on Washington? by Kathleen Krull
King's Courage by Stacia Deutsch and Rhody Cohon

549 BOOK SUGGESTIONS, CONT.

39. A BOOK ABOUT MONEY
The Toothpaste Millionaire by Jean Merrill
Lawn Boy by Gary Paulsen
Sled Dog School by Terry Lynn Johnson
Show Me the Money by Alvin Hall
Nickel Bay Nick by Dean Pitchford
Shoeshine Girl by Clyde Robert Bulla
DK Eyewitness: Money

40. A BOOK ABOUT ART OR ARTISTS
The Chalk Box Kid by Clyde Robert Bulla
The Paint Brush Kid by Clyde Robert Bulla
The Man in the Ceiling by Jules Feiffer
Boys of Steel by Marc Tyler Nobleman
Grandma Moses by Alexandra Wallner
Who Was Claude Monet? by Ann Waldron
Disney's Dream by Stacia Deutsch and Rhody Cohon

41. A BOOK ABOUT MUSIC OR A MUSICIAN
Soldier Song by Debbie Levy
Melody: No Ordinary Sound by Denise Lewis Patrick
Composer series by Anna Harwell Celenza
A Band of Angels by Deborah Hopkinson
The Science of Sound & Music by Shar Levine and Leslie Johnstone
The School of Music by Meurig and Rachel Bowen
Young Mozart by Rachel Isadora
The Story of the Orchestra by Robert Levine
Who Was Wolfgang Amadeus Mozart? by Yona Zeldis McDonough
Blue Ridge Billy by Lois Lenski

42. A BOOK ABOUT AN INVENTION OR INVENTOR
Inventions and Discovery set (Graphic Library)
Robert Fulton: Boy Craftsman by Marguerite Henry
The Story of Eli Whitney by Jean Lee Latham
How Things Are Made by Oldrich Ruzicka
The Boo-Boos That Changed the World by Barry Wittenstein
Electrical Wizard by Elizabeth Rusch
The Inventor's Secret by Suzanne Slade
The Kid Who Invented the Popsicle by Don L. Wulffson
Ben Franklin's Big Splash by Barb Rosenstock
DK Eyewitness: Invention
Bell's Breakthrough by Stacia Deutsch and Rhody Cohon

43. A BOOK OF CRAFTS OR GAMES
101 Ways to Amaze & Entertain by Peter Gross
Sidewalk Chalk by Jamie Kyle McGillian
Cat's Cradle by Anne Akers Johnson
Juggling for the Complete Klutz by John Cassidy and B.C. Rimbeaux
Low-Mess Crafts for Kids by Debbie Chapman
A Kid's Guide to Awesome Duct Tape Projects by Instructables.com
101 Things to Do Outside from Weldon Owen
Acka Backa Boo! by Opal Dunn

Knit, Hook, and Spin by Laurie Carlson
The Daring Book for Girls by Andrea J. Buchanan
The Dangerous Book for Boys by Conn Iggulden

44. A BOOK ABOUT A BOY
Henry Huggins series by Beverly Cleary
Henry Reed series by Keith Robertson
Homer Price by Robert McCloskey
The Whipping Boy by Sid Fleischman
Diary of an Early American Boy by Eric Sloane
San Francisco Boy by Lois Lenski
Harry Miller's Run by David Almond

45. A BOOK ABOUT A GIRL
Melody: Never Stop Singing by Denise Lewis Patrick
American Girl series
Bayou Suzette by Lois Lenski
Emily's Runaway Imagination by Beverly Cleary
The Rose Years series by Roger Lea MacBride
The Caroline Years series by Maria D. Wilkes
The Charlotte Years series by Melissa Wiley
A Gathering of Days by Joan W. Blos
Ruthie's Gift by Kimberly Brubaker Bradley

46. A BOOK ABOUT BOOKS OR A LIBRARY
Schomburg: The Man Who Built a Library by Carole Boston Weatherford
The Tiny Hero of Ferny Creek Library by Linda Bailey
Escape from Mr. Lemoncello's Library by Chris Grabenstein
The Year of the Book by Andrea Cheng
Book Scavenger series by Jennifer Chambliss Bertman
Absolutely Truly by Heather Vogel Frederick
The Mother-Daughter Book Club series by Heather Vogel Frederick
You Wouldn't Want to Live Without Books! by Alex Woolf

47. A BOOK ABOUT ADOPTION
As Simple as It Seems by Sarah Weeks
Penny and Peter by Carolyn Haywood
Here's a Penny by Carolyn Haywood
Pictures of Hollis Woods by Patricia Reilly Giff
All About Adoption by Marc Nemiroff and Jane Annunziata
At Home in This World by Jean MacLeod
Three Names of Me by Mary Cummings
True Colors by Natalie Kinsey-Warnock

48. A BOOK ABOUT SOMEONE WHO IS DIFFERENTLY ABLED
Song for a Whale by Lynne Kelly
Secret Supers by Andy Zach
The Door in the Wall by Marguerite de Angeli
The Summer of the Swans by Betsy Byars
My Brother Charlie by Holly Robinson Peete and Ryan Elizabeth Peete
Helen Keller by Margaret Davidson
El Deafo by Cece Bell
Braille for the Sighted by Jane Schneider
Imagine Being Deaf by Linda O'Neill

49. A BOOK YOU OR YOUR FAMILY OWNS BUT YOU'VE NEVER READ
If you're a responsible person who has read every book in the house, feel free to use a book you've walked past at the library or a book your child has heard people talking about but has never read.

549 BOOK SUGGESTIONS, CONT.

50. A BOOK ABOUT BABIES
The Year of the Baby by Andrea Cheng
Betsy's Little Star by Carolyn Haywood
Lavender by Karen Hesse
Cam Jansen and the Valentine Baby Mystery by David Adler
Iris and Walter and Baby Rose by Elissa Haden Guest
Hank Zipzer: Who Ordered This Baby? Definitely Not Me! by Henry Winkler and Lin Oliver
Here We All Are by Tomie DePaola
The Baby-Sitter's Club series by Ann M. Martin

51. A BOOK ABOUT WRITING
Hero Dog by Hilde Lysiak
The Right Word: Roget and His Thesaurus by Jen Bryant
Idea Jar by Adam Lehrhaupt and Deb Pilutti
How to Write a Book Report by Cecilia Minden and Kate Roth
My Weird Writing Tips by Dan Gutman
Writing Magic by Gail Carson Levine
Spilling Ink by Ellen Potter and Anne Mazer
What Do Authors Do? by Eileen Christelow
Hairy, Scary, Ordinary: What Is an Adjective? by Brian P. Cleary
Make Me Giggle: Writing Your Own Silly Story by Nancy Loewen

52. A BOOK MADE INTO A MOVIE
Because of Winn-Dixie by Kate DiCamillo
Bridge to Terabithia by Katherine Paterson
Charlie and the Chocolate Factory by Roald Dahl
Charlotte's Web by E.B. White
Ella Enchanted by Gail Carson Levine
Chitty Chitty Bang Bang by Ian Fleming
The Hundred and One Dalmatians by Dodie Smith
The Rescuers by Margery Sharp
The Incredible Journey by Sheila Burnford
Pinocchio by Carlo Collodi
Freaky Friday by Mary Rodgers

53. A BOOK ABOUT YOUR STATE OR REGION
You choose! Ask your local library, historical society, or homeschool group for ideas if you're stumped. This could also be a book about your geographical region: the prairie, the forest, the coast. Or it could be about your city.

54. A BOOK RECOMMENDED BY A LIBRARIAN OR TEACHER
Ask your librarian, ballet teacher, karate instructor, French tutor...

55. AN ENCYCLOPEDIA, DICTIONARY, OR ALMANAC
This is unlikely to be a book you'll read cover-to-cover, yet it's definitely a resource you want your child to be familiar with. Consider reading a set number of pages or spending a specified amount of time and then checking it off the list.

The Usborne Children's Encyclopedia
Scholastic Children's Encyclopedia
DK Smithsonian Picturepedia
DK Merriam-Webster's Children's Dictionary

Macmillan First Dictionary by Christopher G. Morris

56. A BOOK ABOUT BUILDING OR ARCHITECTURE
Fallingwater by Marc Harshman & Anna Egan Smucker
How Emily Saved the Bridge by Frieda Wishinsky
The Future Architect's Handbook by Barbara Beck
Cool Architecture by Simon Armstrong
Skyscrapers! Super Structures by Carol Johnman
Architecture According to Pigeons by Speck Lee Tailfeather
Steven Caney's Ultimate Building Book

57. A BIOGRAPHY OF A WORLD LEADER
Peter the Great by Diane Stanley
Franklin and Winston by Douglas Wood
My Brother Martin by Christine King Farris
Who Was Nelson Mandela? by Pam Pollack and Meg Belviso
DK Eyewitness: Gandhi

58. A BOOK PUBLISHED THE SAME YEAR YOUR FOURTH-GRADER WAS BORN
You choose. Stumped? We found that searching for "best childrens' books of 20 ___" provided several lists to browse.

59. A BOOK WITH A ONE-WORD TITLE
Frindle by Andrew Clements
Redwall by Brian Jacques
Shiloh by Phyllis Reynolds Naylor
Scout by Julie Nye

60. A BOOK OR MAGAZINE ABOUT A CAREER YOU'RE INTERESTED IN
Ask someone in that career for recommendations.

61. A BOOK ABOUT SIBLINGS
Caterpillar Summer by Gillian McDunn
The Penderwicks series by Jeanne Birdsall

Treasure Hunters series by James Patterson and Chris Grabenstein
Gone-Away Lake by Elizabeth Enright
From the Mixed-Up Files of Mrs. Basil E. Frankweiler by E.L. Konigsburg
The Moffats by Eleanor Estes

62. A BOOK ABOUT ANIMALS
Heartwood Hotel: A True Home by Kallie George
Rabbit Hill by Robert Lawson
Mountain Born by Elizabeth Yates
Lulu series by Hilary McKay
Gentle Ben by Walt Morey
Rikki-Tikki-Tavi by Rudyard Kipling

63. A BOOK FEATURING A DOG
Ginger Pye by Eleanor Estes
Tippy Lemmey by Patricia C. McKissack
Along Came a Dog by Meindert DeJong
Old Yeller by Fred Gipson
Big Red by Jim Kjelgaard
DK Eyewitness: Dog
Ribsy by Beverly Cleary

549 BOOK SUGGESTIONS, CONT.

64. A BOOK FEATURING A HORSE
Sergeant Reckless by Patricia McCormick
Step Right Up by Donna Janell Bowman
Pony Pals series by Jeanne Betancourt
Misty of Chincoteague and others by Marguerite Henry
The Black Stallion series by Walter Farley
My Friend Flicka by Mary O'Hara
Who Was Seabiscuit? by James Buckley, Jr.
War Horse by Michael Morpurgo
Riding Freedom by Pam Muñoz Ryan
DK Pocket Genius: Horses

65. A BOOK YOU HAVE STARTED BUT NEVER FINISHED
You're looking for a book you set aside just for a little bit while you finished something else or a book that you were too young for at the time so it seemed tedious. Maybe now you're ready!

66. A BOOK ABOUT PLANTS OR GARDENING
The Friendship Garden series by Jenny Meyerhoff
The Vanderbeekers and the Hidden Garden by Karina Yan Glaser
The Year of the Garden by Andrea Cheng
Usborne Gardening for Beginners
Me and the Pumpkin Queen by Marlane Kennedy

67. A BOOK ABOUT A HOBBY OR A SKILL YOU WANT TO LEARN
You choose! Is there something that your child would enjoy learning? From science experiments to building a fort, there's a book for everything. Keep in mind that the skill doesn't have to be feasible to use right away. Choosing a horse or flying a spaceship are fair game!

68. A BOOK OF COMICS
Peanuts by Charles Schulz
Family Circus by Bil Keane
Calvin and Hobbes by Bill Watterson
The Adventures of Tintin by Hergé
Red and Rover by Brian Basset
Garfield series by Jim Davis

69. A BOOK ABOUT A FAMOUS WAR
You Can Fly by Carole Boston Weatherford
My Friend the Enemy by J.B. Cheaney
A Spy Called James by Anne Rockwell
The Black Regiment of the American Revolution by Linda Crotta Brennan
Pink and Say by Patricia Polacco
True Stories of War graphic novels
The Search by Eric Heuvel
A Family Secret by Eric Heuvel
Snow Treasure by Marie McSwigan

Primrose Day by Carolyn Haywood
Twenty and Ten by Claire Huchet Bishop
The World Wars by Paul Dowswell
The Perilous Road by William O. Steele
Shades of Gray by Carolyn Reeder

70. A BOOK ABOUT SPORTS
We Are the Ship by Kadir Nelson
Just Jump! by Mabel Elizabeth Singletary
Something to Prove by Rob Skead
Betsy and the Boys by Carolyn Haywood
King of the Mound by Wes Tooke
Mighty Jackie by Marissa Moss
Dugout Rivals by Fred Bowen
Finding Buck McHenry by Alfred Slote
Baseball in April by Gary Soto
DK Eyewitness: Baseball

71. A BOOK ABOUT MATH
Life of Fred series
A Hundred Billion Trillion Stars by Seth Fishman
Mystery Math by David A. Adler
Sir Cumference series by Cindy Neuschwander
Go Figure! by Johnny Ball
How Many Guinea Pigs Can Fit on a Plane? by Laura Overdeck

72. A BOOK ABOUT SUFFERING OR POVERTY
The Hundred Dresses by Eleanor Estes
Esperanza Rising by Pam Muñoz Ryan
A Letter to Mrs. Roosevelt by C. Coco De Young
Out of the Dust by Karen Hesse
Blue Willow by Doris Gates
Nory Ryan's Song by Patricia Reilly Giff
If Wishes Were Horses by Natalie Kinsey-Warnock
What Was the Great Depression? by Janet B. Pascal
Mama Hattie's Girl by Lois Lenski

73. A BOOK BY YOUR FAVORITE AUTHOR
Your child will choose this one, though you may have to help him think through his favorite books to narrow down the author he's enjoying most right now.

74. A BOOK YOU'VE READ BEFORE
Your child should choose, and make sure you mark it down since it's obviously one he finds interesting!

75. A BOOK WITH AN UGLY COVER
Let your child choose, of course, and make sure to document what he thinks is ugly about it!

76. A BOOK ABOUT SOMEONE ELSE'S FAVORITE SUBJECT
Does your child have a sibling who loves math or painting, a friend enthralled with laws or construction, or perhaps a grandparent who serves as a police officer or NICU nurse? Help him find a book about this subject to enjoy and maybe even share with his friend or relative who inspired this selection!

549 BOOK SUGGESTIONS, CONT.

77. A BOOK ABOUT TRAVEL OR TRANSPORTATION
National Geographic Kids Ultimate U.S. Road Trip Atlas
DK Eyewitness: Car
DK Eyewitness: Train
Lonely Planet Kids: The Travel Book
Wagons Ho! by George Hallowell and Joan Holub
Amelia's Are-We-There-Yet Longest Ever Car Trip by Marissa Moss
Judy's Journey by Lois Lenski
The Red Trailer Mystery by Julie Campbell

78. A BOOK ABOUT THE NATURAL WORLD
Kildee House by Rutherford Montgomery
Nature Anatomy by Julia Rothman
Willa's Wilderness Campout by Valerie Tripp
Owls in the Family by Farley Mowat
A Week in the Woods by Andrew Clements
DK Eyewitness: Natural Disasters

79. A BIOGRAPHY OF AN AUTHOR
A Boy, a Mouse, and a Spider--The Story of E. B. White by Barbara Herkert
Noah Webster's Fighting Words by Tracy Nelson Maurer
Who Was Beatrix Potter? by Sarah Fabiny
Who Was J.R.R. Tolkien? by Pam Pollack
Who Was Charles Dickens? by Pam Pollack
Laura Ingalls Wilder: A Biography by William Anderson

80. A BOOK PUBLISHED IN 2020-2021
Your librarian should be able to point you towards the new releases that are age-appropriate (you may want to preview them, though!) or you can watch to see what's being featured in your favorite book-seller's email or storefront. Of course, you could also expand this category to be any brand-new book or new-to-your-library title.

81. A HISTORICAL FICTION BOOK
All Different Now by Angela Johnson
Thee, Hannah! by Marguerite de Angeli
Calico Bush by Rachel Field
Dear America series from Scholastic
My Name Is America series from Scholastic
We Were There series (various authors, out of print)
A Tale of Gold by Thelma Hatch Wyss

82. A BOOK ABOUT SCIENCE OR A SCIENTIST
Wile E. Coyote, Physical Science Genius series
Max Axiom graphic novels
Superman Science by Agnieszka Biskup
Wells of Knowledge Science series
DK Eyewitness: Science
Galileo's Leaning Tower Experiment by Wendy Macdonald

83. A BOOK ABOUT SAFETY OR SURVIVAL
Do your kids know both when and how to call 911? As landlines become less common, you will want to make sure that your child knows how to access 911 on the actual

devices he has access to every day. You won't see that specifically addressed in these books, but it is worth setting some time aside to discuss this with your child. (BTW, if you accidentally actually dial 911, stay on the line. Every department is different, but here our police department is obligated to investigate every 911 hang-up for obvious reasons. If you stay on the line and explain, that will save everyone some time.)

This is also a great opportunity to visit your local fire and police departments for a tour. Your child will learn a ton about his community, and they often have helpful handouts — for instance, fire escape planning info, etc.

Kids to the Rescue! by Maribeth Boelts
Titan and the Wild Boars: The True Cave Rescue of the Thai Soccer Team by Susan Hood and Pathana Sornhiran
Show Me How to Survive by Joseph Pred
The SOS File by Betsy Byars, Betsy Duffey, and Laurie Myers
I Survived series by Lauren Tarshis
First Aid Basics by Elizabeth Lang

84. A BOOK ABOUT SPACE OR AN ASTRONAUT

DK Pocket Genius: Space
DK Eyewitness: Astronomy
The Challenger Explosion by Heather Adamson
A Child's Introduction to the Night Sky by Michael Driscoll
Reaching for the Moon by Buzz Aldrin
I Love You, Michael Collins by Lauren Baratz-Logsted
Hidden Figures - Young Reader's Edition by Margot Lee Shetterly
Neil Armstrong: Young Flyer by Montrew Dunham
What's Inside a Black Hole? by Andrew Solway
NASA Mathematician Katherine Johnson by Heather E. Schwartz

85. A BOOK SET IN CENTRAL OR SOUTH AMERICA

A Kid's Guide to Latino History by Valerie Petrillo
Secret of the Andes by Ann Nolan Clark
Chucaro: Wild Pony of the Pampa by Francis Kalnay
The Corn Grows Ripe by Dorothy Rhoads
The Dragon Slayer by Jaime Hernandez
The Amazing Mexican Secret by Jeff Brown and Macky Pamintuan
Where Is Machu Picchu? by Megan Stine

86. A BOOK SET IN AFRICA

A Girl of Two Worlds by Lorna Eglin
Beat the Story-Drum, Pum-Pum by Ashley Bryan
Cooking the East African Way by Bertha Vining Montgomery
The African Safari Discovery by Jeff Brown and Macky Pamintuan
A Girl Named Disaster by Nancy Farmer

87. A BOOK SET IN ASIA

Tiger Boy by Mitali Perkins
Mei Fuh: Memories from China by Edith Schaeffer
We Visit China by Joanne Mattern
Little One-Inch and Other Japanese Children's Favorite Stories compiled by Florence Sakade
The Land I Lost by Quang Nhuong Huynh
The Flying Chinese Wonders by Jeff Brown and Macky Pamintuan
Where Is the Great Wall? by Patricia Brennan Demuth

549 BOOK SUGGESTIONS, CONT.

88. A BOOK SET IN EUROPE
Red Sails to Capri by Ann Weil
The Martha Years series by Melissa Wiley
The House on Walenska Street by Charlotte Herman
Bloomability by Sharon Creech
The Squire's Tales series by Gerald Morris
Framed in France by Jeff Brown and Macky Pamintuan

89. A BOOK WITH A COLOR IN ITS TITLE
White Stallion of Lipizza by Marguerite Henry
The Green Glass Sea by Ellen Klages
The Red Fairy Book and others by Andrew Lang
The Green Ember by S.D. Smith
Pinky Pye by Eleanor Estes
Encyclopedia Brown series by Donald J. Sobol

90. A BOOK ABOUT MANNERS
Emily Post's the Guide to Good Manners for Kids
A Kid's Guide to Manners by Katherine Flannery
A Smart Girl's Guide: Manners by Nancy Holyoke
Dude, That's Rude! by Pamela Espeland and Elizabeth Verdick

91. A BOOK ABOUT SPRING
Spring According to Humphrey by Betty G. Birney
The Riddle of the Robin by Valerie Tripp
The Penderwicks in Spring by Jeanne Birdsall
The Marshland Mystery by Kathryn Kenny

92. A BOOK ABOUT SUMMER
One Crazy Summer by Rita Williams-Garcia
A Promise and a Rainbow by Mabel Elizabeth Singletary
The Season of Styx Malone by Kekla Magoon
Summer According to Humphrey by Betty G. Birney

Thimble Summer by Elizabeth Enright
The Penderwicks: A Summer Tale... by Jeanne Birdsall
Love, Ruby Lavender by Deborah Wiles
Houseboat Girl by Lois Lenski
The Secret of the Mansion by Julie Campbell
Surprise Island by Gertrude Chandler Warner

93. A BOOK ABOUT AUTUMN
The Friendship Garden: Pumpkin Spice by Jenny Meyerhoff
If You Were at the First Thanksgiving by Anne Kamma
The Muddily-Puddily Show by Valerie Tripp
The Mystery off Glen Road by Julie Campbell
Cotton in My Sack by Lois Lenski

94. A BOOK ABOUT WINTER
Pugs of the Frozen North by Philip Reeve
Winter According to Humphrey by Betty G. Birney
The Mystery of Mr. E by Valerie Tripp
The Winter Rescue by Paul Hutchens
Snowflake Bentley by Jacqueline Briggs Martin
The Long Winter by Laura Ingalls Wilder
The Black Jacket Mystery by Kathryn Kenny
Snowbound Mystery by Gertrude Chandler Warner
The Happy Hollisters at Snowflake Camp by Jerry West

95. A BOOK FROM THE 000-099 DEWEY DECIMAL SECTION OF YOUR LIBRARY
Books about computer science, information, and general works

96. A BOOK FROM THE 100-199 DEWEY DECIMAL SECTION OF YOUR LIBRARY
Books about philosophy and psychology

97. A BOOK FROM THE 200-299 DEWEY DECIMAL SECTION OF YOUR LIBRARY
Books about religion

98. A BOOK FROM THE 300-399 DEWEY DECIMAL SECTION OF YOUR LIBRARY
Books about social sciences

99. A BOOK FROM THE 400-499 DEWEY DECIMAL SECTION OF YOUR LIBRARY
Books about language

100. A BOOK FROM THE 500-599 DEWEY DECIMAL SECTION OF YOUR LIBRARY
Books about science

101. A BOOK FROM THE 600-699 DEWEY DECIMAL SECTION OF YOUR LIBRARY
Books about technology

102. A BOOK FROM THE 700-799 DEWEY DECIMAL SECTION OF YOUR LIBRARY
Books about arts and recreation

103. A BOOK FROM THE 800-899 DEWEY DECIMAL SECTION OF YOUR LIBRARY
Books about literature

104. A BOOK FROM THE 900-999 DEWEY DECIMAL SECTION OF YOUR LIBRARY
Books about history and geography

Book Awards & Party!

DO THIS AS SOON AS YOU FINISH YOUR READING CHALLENGE!

Grab your child's reading list from pages 28–33 and help him fill out the awards page (opposite page) to give his best and worst books an official award and mark them as most memorable this year.

Encourage him not to agonize over "was this one really the best..." but to go with his general impressions or write down all the contenders.

Send us a copy of this at books@timberdoodle.com and we'll be thrilled to credit you 50 Doodle Dollar Reward points (worth $2.50 off your next order) as our thank you for taking the time to share. We'll also congratulate your child on a job so well done!

Bonus Idea
Have an "awards ceremony" night all about one of the books on your list! You'll get the most specific ideas by searching online for "*book I picked* theme party," but here are some things to think through as you get started.

Food: How can you tie the menu to the theme? A book like Green Eggs and Ham or Pancakes for Breakfast or is easy—just replicate the food in the book! If you're working with a book that doesn't feature food directly there are a few options. Perhaps the book featured a construction crew—you could all eat from "lunchboxes" tonight or set up your kitchen to masquerade as a food truck. Or, if you're reading a book about the pioneers, do a little research and eat frying pan bread, beans, venison, and cornmeal mush.

You could also take the food you would normally eat and reshape it to match your story. For instance, sandwiches can be cut into ships, round apple slices can be life preservers, crackers can be labeled "hard tack," and you're well on your way to a party featuring your favorite nautical tale.

Don't forget the setting, too. As ridiculous as it sounds, eating dinner by (battery-operated!) lantern light under your table draped with blankets will make that simple camping tale an experience your family will be recalling for years to come.

Or perhaps some handmade red table fans, softly playing traditional Chinese music, and a red tablecloth would provide the perfect backdrop for the story about life in China.

The more senses you use, the more memorable you make this experience. Use appropriate background music, diffuse peppermint oil to make it smell like Christmas, dim the lights, eat at the top of the playground, or whatever would set this apart from a regular night and make it just a bit crazy and fun.

Don't get trapped in either the "we must do this tonight" mode or in the "we can't do this because it won't be perfect" mode. Allowing your child to spend a few days creating decorations and menus is wonderful! Doing it today because it's the only free night on the horizon even though you can only integrate a few ideas into the preset menu? Also amazing! Your goal is to value the book and make some fun memories.

BOOK AWARDS OF

(YOUR CHILD'S NAME HERE ^)   (YEAR HERE ^)

I READ ____ BOOKS FROM THE READING CHALLENGE THIS YEAR!

FUNNIEST BOOK:

MOST MEMORABLE BOOK:

BOOK I READ THE MOST TIMES:

BOOK I ENJOYED LEAST:

TEACHER'S FAVORITE BOOK:

BOOK I MOST WISH WAS A SERIES:

CHOOSE YOUR OWN AWARD:

YOUR TOP 4 FAQ ABOUT NEXT YEAR
THINGS TO THINK THROUGH AS YOU ANTICIPATE FIFTH GRADE

So, you're finishing up fourth grade already? How has it gone for you? Really, we'd love to know! (Plus, you get reward points for your review.) Just jump over to the Fourth-Grade Nonreligious Curriculum on our website and scroll down to submit a review.

As you look toward next year, there are a few things that you may want to know.

1. When Can We See the New Kits?
New kits usually release in April. Check our Facebook or give us a call for this year's projection, but it's always in the spring and usually April. Each year discontinued items are replaced, and any spectacular new items are added. It is rare to change significant parts of the scope and sequence for a grade, but it's common to add little bits of "wow" that we've been busy all year finding.

2. Free Customization
If your child has raced ahead in some subjects this year, or if you've realized you need to go back and fill in some gaps, or if you simply don't need more Math-U-See blocks, you'll be thrilled to know that you can customize your kit next year to accommodate that. You'll find full details on our website, but know that it is free and can often be completed online if you prefer to DIY.

3. Do I Need to Take the Summer Off?

Some students finish the grade with an eager passion to jump right into the next grade, and parents contact us asking if that's really okay or if they should take some time off so the child doesn't burn out. We are year-round homeschoolers, so we would definitely be fans of jumping into the next grade here!

However, the truth is that this is a decision only you can make. We can tell you that a long break can quench the thirst for knowledge, so if it were our child, we'd seriously consider moving right into the next grade. However, sometimes a little suspense makes the year begin with a beautiful anticipation!

If you decide to start early, you could consider saving one or two items for your official start date so that there is still some anticipation.

4. Can I Refill This Kit for My Next Child?

Absolutely! Each year's Additional Student Kit reflects the current year's kit (so the 2020-2021 Fourth-Grade Elite Kit and the 2020-2021 Additional Student Kit correlate). If you love it just the way it is, refill it now before we swap things around for next year. Or, if you prefer, wait for the new kits to launch and then let our team help you figure out what tweaks (if any) need to be made to the standard Additional Student Kit.

We're Here to Help!

If you have other questions for us, would like to share additional feedback, or would like to get in touch for some other reason, don't hesitate to drop us a line or give us a call. (FYI, we also have online chat on our website, in case that's easier for you.)

mail@Timberdoodle.com
800-478-0672
360-426-0672

Doodle Dollar Reward Points

WHAT THEY ARE, HOW THEY WORK, AND WHERE TO FIND THEM

If you're one of our Charter School BFFs, we just want to give you a heads up that the following information doesn't really apply to you. Doodle Dollars are earned on individual prepaid (credit cards or online payment plans are fine) orders and don't apply to purchase orders or school district orders. Sorry about that!

Now, with that out of the way, here's the good news. Almost any item you order directly from us earns you reward points! You will earn 1 point for every $1 you spend. 20 points = $1 off a future order!

Some families prefer to use this money as they go, while others save it up for Christmas or for those mid-year purchases that just weren't in the budget.

Can I Earn More Points?
Absolutely! Review your purchases on Timberdoodle.com to earn points. Add pictures for even more points!

We also usually have a few reward point events throughout the year, as well as our year-round Doodle Crew opportunities.

What Can I Spend My Points On?
Anything on our website. These reward points act as a gift certificate to be used on anything you like.

How Do I Get to My Points?
The simplest way is to look for the teal Doodle Dollars pop-up in the lower left corner of our website. Click it, login, then click All Rewards > Redeem and drag the slider to determine how many points to cash out. You'll immediately be issued a gift certificate to apply to your order. If you run into any challenges, please let our team know and we will be thrilled to assist you.

Check our website for the latest information on reward points:
www.Timberdoodle.com/doodledollars